Prisoner
Without a Name,
Cell
Without a Number

Prisoner Without a Name, Cell Without a Number

Jacobo Timerman

Translated from the Spanish by
Toby Talbot

WEIDENFELD AND NICOLSON   LONDON

To

MARSHALL MEYER

A rabbi who brought comfort to Jewish, Christian, and atheist prisoners in Argentine jails

Foreword

My father was Nathan Timerman. Nathan ben Jacob (Nathan, son of Jacob). And I am Jacob ben Nathan. Jacob, named after my father's father. The Timermans, by way of those strange, biforked paths of Judaism, escaped the Spanish occupation of the Netherlands, and the Inquisition, and wound up in a small town of Vinnitsa Oblast in the Ukraine, called Bar. Family accounts, rather imprecise and often colored by vanity, claim that the Timermans were prominent in the community and fought for Jewish rights.

It was, most likely, an enlightened, combative community inasmuch as the Jews of Bar, by 1556, had reached an agreement with their townsmen that allowed them to own buildings and granted them the same rights and obligations as the other residents, including travel to other cities in the district for family or business reasons.

When the Cossack chief Chmielnitski passed through Bar in 1648–49, he of course massacred all the Jews he could capture. The community recovered, however, and assumed that something as brutal as the existence of Cossack murderers could only be God's final test before the coming of the Messiah. So staunch was their conviction that in 1717 they constructed their Great Synagogue, receiving permission

beforehand from the bishop. I attended that synagogue with
my father, his six brothers, and all my cousins, and bear
within me still a vague longing for those tall, bearded, un-
smiling men.

In 1941, when the Nazis entered Bar, they set that synagogue on fire, burning many Jews to death. All the other Jews
of Bar plus others from the environs, including the Timermans, who had survived the sufferings—which according to
their rabbis had been imposed by God to herald the Messiah's
arrival—were killed by the Nazis in October of 1942. Some
twelve thousand within a couple of days. My father, happily,
had left Bar for Argentina in 1928.

In 1977, in Argentina, the same ideological conviction that
impelled Chmielnitski and the Nazis reverberated in the
questions posed by my interrogators inside the army's clandestine prisons.

And in their methods of torture as well.

But I have survived, to give testimony. And I'm doing so,
at age fifty-seven, in the land of Israel, where I'm beginning
this book a few days after the birth of the first Israeli Timerman, whose name is Nahum ben Nathan ben Jacob. That is,
Nahum (he who brings solace), son of Nathan, who is the son
of Jacob, who is the son of that other Nathan in Bar who was
the son of Jacob, whose grave he left when departing for
Argentina.

We have completed our voyage.

J.T.
Tel Aviv
January–July 1980

Prisoner
Without a Name,
Cell
Without a Number

1

The cell is narrow. When I stand at its center, facing the steel door, I can't extend my arms. But it is long, and when I lie down, I can stretch out my entire body. A stroke of luck, for in the cell I previously occupied—for how long?—I was forced to huddle up when seated and keep my knees bent while lying down.

The cell is quite high. When I jump, I'm unable to touch the ceiling. The white walls have been recently painted. Undoubtedly they once had names on them, messages, words of encouragement, dates. They are now bereft of any vestige or testimony.

The floor of the cell is permanently wet. Somewhere there's a leak. The mattress is also wet. I have a blanket, and to prevent that from getting wet I keep it on my shoulders constantly. If I lie down with the blanket on top of me, the part of my body touching the mattress gets soaked. I discover it's best to roll up the mattress so that one part of it doesn't touch the ground. In time, the top part dries. This means, though, that I can't lie down, but must sleep seated. My life goes on during this period—for how long?—either standing or seated.

The cell has a steel door with an opening that allows part

of a face, a minimal part, to be visible. The guard has orders to keep the opening shut. Light enters from the outside through a small crack, which acts also as an air vent. This is the only ventilation and light. A faint glow, night and day, eliminating time. Producing a semi-penumbra within an atmosphere of contaminated air, semi-air.

I miss my former cell—where was that?—because it had a hole in the ground into which to urinate and defecate. In my present one I must call the guard to take me to the bathroom. It's a complicated procedure, and they're not always in the mood. It requires that they open a door, the entrance to the ward where my cell is located, close it from the inside, announce that they're about to open the door of my cell in order for me to turn my back to it, blindfold my eyes, guide me toward the bathroom, and bring me back, reversing the whole procedure. It amuses them sometimes to tell me that I'm alongside the latrine when I am not. Or to guide me— by one hand, or shoving me from behind—so that I stick one foot into the latrine. Eventually they tire of this game and don't respond to my call. I do it on myself. Which is why I miss the cell with the hole in it.

I do it on myself. And then must get special permission to have my clothes washed and must wait in the cell, naked, until they're dry and are brought back to me. Sometimes days pass because—they claim—it's raining. My isolation is so overwhelming that I prefer to believe what I'm told. Still, I miss the cell with the hole in it.

The discipline of the guards is not very good. Often one will bring food to me without blindfolding my eyes. Then I can see his face. He smiles. Sentry duty wearies them, for they must also serve as torturers, interrogators, and perform the duties of kidnappers. They're the only ones functioning in these clandestine prisons. On the other hand, they're entitled to part of the booty in every arrest. One of the guards has my watch. During an interrogation another guard offered me a cigarette and lit it with my wife's lighter. I later learned that they were under army orders not to steal any-

thing from my house throughout the kidnapping but suc-
cumbed to temptation. Gold Rolex watches and Dupont cigarette lighters were almost an obsession with the Argentine
security forces during that year of 1977.

Tonight, a guard, not following the rules, leaves the peephole
ajar. I wait a while to see what will happen but it remains
open. Standing on tiptoe, I peer out. There's a narrow corridor, and across from my cell I can see at least two other doors.
Indeed, I have a full view of two doors. What a sensation of
freedom! An entire universe added to my Time, that elon-
gated time which hovers over me oppressively in the cell.
Time, that dangerous enemy of man, when its existence,
duration, and eternity are virtually palpable.

The light in the corridor is strong. Momentarily blinded, I
step back, then hungrily return. I try to fill myself with the
visible space. So long have I been deprived of a sense of
distance and proportion that I feel suddenly unleashed. In
order to look out, I must lean my face against the icy steel
door. As the minutes pass, the cold becomes unbearable. My
entire forehead is pressed against the steel and the cold
makes my head ache. But it's been a long time—how long?
—without a celebration of space. I press my ear against the
door, yet hear no sound. I resume looking.

He is doing the same. I suddenly realize that the peephole
in the door facing mine is also open and that there's an eye
behind it. I'm startled: They've laid a trap for me. Looking
through the peephole is forbidden and they've seen me
doing it. I step back and wait. I wait for some Time, more
Time, and again more Time. And then return to the peephole.

He is doing the same.

And now I must talk about you, about that long night we
spent together, during which you were my brother, my fa-

ther, my son, my friend. Or, are you a woman? If so, we passed that night as lovers. You were merely an eye, yet you too remember that night, don't you? Later, I was told that you'd died, that you had a weak heart and couldn't survive the "machine," but they didn't mention whether you were a man or a woman. How can you have died, considering that that night we conquered death?

You must remember, I need you to remember, for otherwise I'm obliged to remember for us both, and the beauty we experienced requires your testimony as well. You blinked. I clearly recall you blinking. And that flutter of movement proved conclusively that I was not the last human survivor on earth amid this universe of torturing custodians. At times, inside my cell, I'd move an arm or a leg merely to view a movement that was nonviolent, that differed from the ones employed when I was dragged or pushed by the guards. And you blinked. It was beautiful.

You were—you are?—a person of high human qualities, endowed certainly with a profound knowledge of life, for you invented all sorts of games that night, creating Movement in our confined world. You'd suddenly move away, then return. At first I was frightened. But then I realized you were re-creating the great human adventure of lost-and-found—and I played the game with you. Sometimes we'd return to the peephole at the same time, and our sense of triumph was so powerful we felt immortal. We were immortal.

I was frightened a second time when you disappeared for a long interval. Desperately I pressed against the peephole, my forehead frozen on that cold night—it was night, wasn't it?—and I took off my shirt and propped it under my forehead. When you returned I was furious, and you undoubtedly saw my fury for you didn't disappear again. This must have been a great effort for you. A few days later, when taken for a session with the "machine," I heard one guard comment to another about his having used your crutches for kindling. I'm sure that you're aware, though, that such ruses were often used to soften up a prisoner before a "machine" session—a chat with Susan, as they called it. And I didn't believe them. I swear to you I didn't believe them. No one could destroy for me the mutual immortality created during that night of love and comradeship.

You were—you are?—extremely intelligent. Only one possible outgoing act would have occurred to me: looking out, looking, ceaselessly looking. But you unexpectedly stuck your chin in front of the peephole. Then your mouth, or part of your forehead. I was very desperate. And frightened. I remained glued to the peephole, but only in order to peer out of it. I tried, I assure you, even if briefly, to put my cheek to the opening, whereupon the inside of my cell sprang into view and my spirits immediately dropped. The gap between life and solitude was so evident; knowing that you were nearby, I couldn't bear gazing back toward my cell. You forgave me for this, retaining your vitality and mobility. I realized that you were consoling me, and I started to cry. In silence, of course. You needn't worry. I knew that I couldn't risk uttering a sound. You saw me crying, though, didn't you? You did see that. It did me good, crying in front of you. You know how dismal it is to be in a cell and to say to yourself, It's time to cry a bit, whereupon you cry hoarsely, wretchedly, heedlessly. With you I was able to cry serenely, peacefully, as if allowed to cry. As if everything might be poured into that sobbing, converting it into a prayer rather than tears. You can't imagine how I detested that fitful sobbing of mine inside the cell. That night, you taught me how we could be comrades-in-tears.

I don't know why, but I'm sure that you are—that you were?—a young man of medium height. Let's say thirty-five years old, with a great sense of humor. A few days later a guard came to my cell to soften me up. He gave me a cigarette: it was his turn to play the good guy. He advised me to spill everything, told me that he'd had plenty of experience and that a person my age winds up dying in Susan's arms because his heart can't withstand the electric shocks for long. And he informed me that you'd been "cooled out." This is how he put it: "Look, Jacobo, the only obligation you have is to survive. Politics change. You'll be getting out, you Jews help one another. You'll make a fortune again. You have children. In the cell facing yours there was a crazy guy. We cooled him out. Look, Jacobo . . ."

I didn't believe him. If I was able to withstand it, certainly you were. Did you have a weak heart? Impossible. You were strong-hearted, generous, brave. Such hearts are not destroyed by Susan. Do you remember once how the lights went off? Do you know what I did? I sat down on the mattress, wrapped myself in the blanket, and pretended to sleep. I was very frightened. Suddenly I realized that I hadn't put on my shirt. I did so hastily. But the lights went on again. And I remembered that the guards sometimes amused themselves by turning the lights off and on. It's possible, of course, that a large amount of current was being consumed by Susan. Undoubtedly several new prisoners had arrived, and the first thing automatically done to them was to put them through the machine, even before they were asked who they were. The prisoner's first sensation had to be a session of electric shocks in order to lower his defenses on admittance. I found out later that this technique was changed after some individuals were cooled out before they could even be questioned. Not even the doctor on duty—by the way, do you remember how that doctor kept letting his beard grow, then after a few weeks would shave it off, then let his mustache grow, then only his sideburns, then he'd wear his hair long, then short, all because he was so scared of being identified? —no, not even the doctor was always able to save them.

Yet both of us survived. Do you remember when I got a cramp in my leg while they were torturing me and suddenly my outcries ceased? They thought I had "gone," and were alarmed. They had orders to get me to confess because they wanted to build a big case around me. I wasn't any use to them dead. Yes, I was paralyzed for a moment due to the cramp. It's curious how one can experience pain and joy simultaneously. Although my eyes were blindfolded, I sensed their fear—and rejoiced. Then I began moaning again on account of Susan.

No, I don't think you remember this, though I tried to tell you about it. Yet your eye was much more expressive than mine. I tried to convey the episode to you, for it was as if a battle had been won against them. But at that point I was terribly confused, and it's possible that I meant to tell it to you without actually having done so.

My friend, my brother, how much I learned that night from you. According to my calculations, it must have been April or May of 1977. Suddenly you put your nose in front of the peephole and rubbed it. It was a caress, wasn't it? Yes, a caress. You'd already incorporated so many levels of experience into our captivity, yet persisted in the restoration of our humanity. At that moment you were suggesting tenderness, caressing your nose, gazing at me. You repeated it several times. A caress, then your eye. Another caress, and your eye. You may have thought that I didn't understand. But we understood each other from the start. I knew clearly you were telling me that tenderness would reappear. I don't know why you felt the urgency that night to affirm the equal importance, or even greater importance, of tenderness over love. Is it because tenderness contains an element of resignation, and perhaps that night you were feeling resigned? Is it because tenderness is consoling to someone already resigned? Tenderness is indeed a consolation, whereas love is a need. And you assuredly needed to be consoled. I didn't understand that, but you, my brother, my friend, my companion-in-tears, were you already aware of this and resigned to it? If so, why and for whom am I uttering all these inanities? Am I babbling to myself like a fool? Is there no eye gazing at me?

At dawn one morning in April 1977, some twenty civilians besieged my apartment in midtown Buenos Aires. They said they were obeying orders from the Tenth Infantry Brigade of the First Army Corps. The following day my wife sought information at the First Army Corps and was informed that they knew nothing of my whereabouts.

They uprooted our telephone lines, took possession of our automobile keys, handcuffed me from behind. They covered my head with a blanket, rode down with me to the basement, removed the blanket, and asked me to point out my automobile. They threw me to the floor in the back of the car, covered me with the blanket, stuck their feet on top of me, and jammed into me what felt like the butt of a gun.

No one spoke.

We arrived at a certain place. A pair of large doors opened up. They squeaked. Dogs barked quite close by. Someone said, "I feel fulfilled." I was taken out of the car and flung onto the ground.

A long interval elapsed. I could hear only footsteps. Suddenly, some bursts of laughter. Someone approached and placed what seemed to be the barrel of a revolver against my head. He put one hand on my head and from up close, perhaps leaning over me, said, "I'm going to count to ten. Say goodbye, Jacobo dear. It's all up with you." I said nothing. Again he spoke: "Don't you want to say your prayers?" I said nothing. He started to count.

His voice was well modulated, what you might call an educated voice. He counted slowly, enunciating clearly. It was a pleasant voice. I remained silent, wondering:

"Was it inevitable for me to die like this? Yes, it was inevitable. Was it what I desired? Yes, it was what I desired. Wife, children, I love you. Adiós, adiós, adiós. . . ."

". . . Ten." Ha . . . ha . . . ha! I heard laughter. I too began laughing. Loudly. Great guffaws.

The blindfold is removed from my eyes. I'm in a large, dimly lit study: there's a desk, chairs. Colonel Ramón J. Camps, chief of police of the province of Buenos Aires, is observing me. He orders my arms, handcuffed behind my back, to be freed. This takes a while because the keys have been misplaced. Or, again, it may have taken only a few minutes. He orders a glass of water to be brought to me.

"Timerman," he says, "your life depends on how you answer my questions."

"Without preliminary trial, Colonel?"

"Your life depends on your answers."

"Who ordered my arrest?"

"You're a prisoner of the First Army Corps in action."

2

For a long while one could presume, with goodwill and a measure of liberalism, that Lenin had forecast Russia's future and the Socialist structure in conformance with the way in which it was materializing. Stalin's death, Khrushchev's speech at the 20th Party Congress, and information about the existence of the Gulags all indicated that the more logical point of reference for the Russian reality might still be Dostoyevsky. Something similar transpired in Argentina: suddenly all information and inquiries regarding its history and its present, all predictions as to its future, crystallized in a relatively short book, a curious novel of the late 1920s by Roberto Arlt, entitled *The Seven Madmen*.

The central idea of the novel—reached by way of endless ideological, mystical, political, emotional, and tango-inspired elaborations—found appeal among every violent Argentine group, as well as among Perónist supporters. In it, Arlt brought together seven madmen, ruled by a revolutionary-without-ideology called The Astrologer, whose mission it is to initiate the anarchist-socialist revolution in Argentina and to extend it throughout Latin America via terrorist groups financed by the profits from a chain of brothels. The simplicity of the device is attractive, and recurrent in all totalitarian

ideology: to ignore the complexities of reality, or even eliminate reality, and instead establish a simple goal and a simple
means of attaining that goal.

Curiously enough, Argentine politics during the last fifty
years has in a sense been governed by this equation, applied
in extravagant ideological formulas. Argentina's democratic
parties attempted compromise in order to avoid being swept
aside by the Perónist landslide—a union and electoral mass
that was decisive in elections, when elections took place, and,
more often, created the climate for military overthrow of
those legitimately elected.

Clearly, such a thesis is impossible to accept. It is also
strangely hard to understand or explain. And it has perhaps
turned Argentina into the invalid of Latin America, its ailment akin to that of the Balkans in Europe—an ailment so
unique that the world has long delayed attempting any reaction to it and all such attempts to date have been focused on
marginal aspects rather than on the fundamental issues.

Between 1973 and 1976 there were four Perónist presidents, including General Juan Domingo Perón and his wife
Isabel. The violence enveloping the country erupted on all
fronts, completing a development that had begun in 1964
with the appearance of the first guerrillas, trained in Cuba by
one of Che Guevara's aides-de-camp. Coexisting in Argentina were: rural and urban Trotskyite guerrillas; right-wing
Perónist death squads; armed terrorist groups of the large
labor unions, used for handling union matters; paramilitary
army groups, dedicated to avenging the murder of their
men; para-police groups of both the Left and the Right vying
for supremacy within the organization of federal and provincial police forces; and terrorist groups of Catholic rightists
organized by cabals who opposed Pope John XXIII's propos-
als to reconcile the liberal leftist Catholic priests seeking to
apply—generally·with anarchistic zeal—the ideological thesis of rapprochement between the Church and the poor.
(These, of course, were only the principal groups of organized or systematized violence. Hundreds of other organiza-

tions involved in the eroticism of violence existed, small units that found ideological justification for armed struggle in a poem by Neruda or an essay by Marcuse. Lefebvre might be as useful as Heidegger; a few lines by Mao Zedong might trigger off the assassination of a businessman in a Buenos Aires suburb; and a hazy interpretation of Mircea Eliade might be perfect for kidnapping an industrialist to óbtain a ransom that would make possible a further perusal of Indian philosophy and mysticism to corroborate the importance of national liberation.)

In this climate, which dragged on for years, I conducted two interviews that illustrate Argentina's impotence in finding adequate political responses to that most elemental of needs, survival. One was with a Perónist senator, highly influential in his party, a lawyer, a moderate, a student leader in his youth, a man cultivated and serene. In the United States, he would have been found in the liberal sector of the Democratic Party; in Israel, I imagine he would have been a pillar of the Labor Party; in France, he might have belonged to Giscard's liberal wing. Our conversation revolved around violence—the year was 1975—and I explained to him, with ample statistics and thirty years of experience in political journalism, that the country was heading inevitably toward occupation by military power. I maintained that the only recourse left for preserving the existing political institutions was to make use of legal channels in order to put an end to all brands of violence, and that the army was the only group in a position to do this. I proposed that he, along with the Perónist majority in the Senate and the House of Deputies, should pass extraordinary legislation empowering the army to initiate measures against terrorist activity of all sorts, but that these powers should be limited by congressional statute within the constitutional framework, and should always remain under constant civil jurisdiction.

His reply went as follows: "Once we allow the military to step through the door, they'll take possession of the entire house. This would be tantamount to a coup, leaving us on the outside. Furthermore, right-wing Perónists who support rightist terrorist groups that assassinate leftist Perónists will not vote for the laws; and leftist Perónists who support leftist terrorists who assassinate rightist Perónists will not vote for the laws. Moreover, the army will suppress only one sector of violence and not the other. It will pit one against the other, thus assuring its own survival." And the conclusion? "Let's leave things the way they are. Something will happen. God is Argentine."

The second interview was with a high-ranking official in the Army General Staff. His reply was essentially the same, with only superficial differences. When I asked what were the army's reasons for not using all its resources to combat violence, why it was concerned solely with retaliation for its own casualties, his reply was simple: "Do you expect us to go out and fight so that they [the Perónists] can continue to govern?" The Perónists had won the election with seventy percent of the vote.

Curiously, those long years of violence and extermination in Argentina, during which 10,000 people certainly perished and 15,000 others disappeared, constituted for Argentine leaders of all political leanings a gymnasium in terms of tactics and strategy, an exercise in opportunistic positions. But they were never perceived as a fundamental problem that had to be faced, as a grave peril undermining the very existence of the nation.

It is essential, I suppose, to attempt some explanation of what Argentina is. Yet I find it almost impossible to do so in normal terms, applying current political principles. The problem is not merely that I find it difficult to explain Argentina in comprehensible terms to outsiders, but that I myself perhaps am unable to understand her. Or it may be that I've lived through a period of such political and social disintegration that it is hard for me to conceive that some coherent explanation would emerge from such disparate and anarchistic opposing elements.

In this context, a statement by the Argentine writer Jorge

Luis Borges is, I think, useful. Borges remarked, some thirty years ago, that the Argentine is not a citizen but an inhabitant; that he lacks an idea of the nation where he resides, but views it as a territory which, owing to its wealth, can be exploited rapidly.

To my mind, this is a noteworthy comment on the Argentine problem. Nothing simple: Argentina as an entity does not yet exist; it must be created. But were I to assess how each of the diverse Argentinas existing at present within that territory—each regarding itself as the authentic one—would interpret Borges's definition, that would provide a more descriptive and precise response, something akin to a French pointillistic canvas.

1. If Borges were to comment on his own definition, he would say that the Argentines' error stems from their inadequate understanding of ancient Germanic literature. Borges would claim that it's impossible to create a citizen unless he has read the books of the Veda or at least the Egyptian Mummy's Prayer, which is recited prior to one's admittance as a sacred mummy—in the French version rendered by the Lithuanian poet Lubicz Milosz. Borges would say (in fact, he has said) that "Democracy is an abuse of statistics." In the end, he himself might not understand, or attempt to understand, the value of his own definition.

2. Right-wing sectors would accept Borges's remark as an absolute truth, claiming that it was the flood of immigrants that was responsible for the destruction of the roots implanted by the Spanish monarchy—those Hispanic roots of the noble Bourbons and of Franco—immigrants who came merely to get rich, to "make" America. It was they who prevented consolidation of a notion of citizenry.

3. Liberal sectors would accept Borges's remark as an absolute truth, claiming that it was the incapacity of the Argentine ruling class to understand the immigrant phenomenon —with all its contributions to creativity, culture, the republican and democratic spirit, its impulse toward civic activity, the struggle for human rights and man's equality—and, spe-

cifically, the battle of the r
unlimited immigrant acce
above all political life, th
tion, and hence the cr

4. Leftist sectors wc
lute truth, claiming
he's a citizen withi
geois nation can e
common interests.

5. Fascist sectors would ac
lute truth, claiming that citizens
power organizes them as such, and t
central power, which is required to give e
one, that is lacking in Argentina.

I could go on indefinitely, covering the vagaries
infinite number of ideologies scattered throughout Arge.
tina. Each would accept Borges's statement as a logical, coherent explanation. That, of course, would be their only
point of agreement.

Does this in any way clarify the Argentine drama? This
vignette revolving around Borges, and closely resembling a
Borges story, is actually a perfect embodiment of Argentina's
capacity for violence, as well as its *political incapacity.* What
is more, it reveals that only nations capable of creating a
political environment that embraces multiple political solutions for any situation are able to escape Argentina's violence. No one is immune to episodes of violence and terrorism; yet it should be possible at least to avoid a situation in
which terrorism and violence are the sole creative potential,
the sole imaginative, emotional, erotic expression of a nation.

In a session of the Argentine Parliament, Carlos Perette, a
centrist senator and an anti-Perónist, declared in a speech
following one of the many daily murders: "In Argentina you
know who dies, but not who kills." Could it possibly have
been otherwise? The dead were found thrown into the
streets, and identified. But as for killing, everyone was killing,
and to identify the killers publicly, as you did privately,

ing yourself to death as well. In an article
in reply to that senator, who had shown
ge simply by that innocent, innocuous remark
ess other political leaders, I stated that the only
uired would be for a congressman within the sanc-
the House or Senate to repeat the names that had
uttered in the corridors of Congress, for that would
e public identification of the murderers. But would that
e changed things? I suppose not.

We organized a group of political and labor journalists at
my newspaper, *La Opinión*. We held a meeting to analyze
the situation and decided that hope still existed; we merely
had to begin the battle and explain everything. That day we
wound up toasting each other for having committed ourselves, a true privilege for any civilized man—the privilege
of combating fascism. I recall having said something to the
following effect: "Our generation witnessed the struggle
against fascism during World War II only through the street
demonstrations that took place in Buenos Aires. We ran no
risk. Nor did we run any of the risks faced by those confronting Stalinism and languishing now in the Gulags. We're lucky
at least to be here, with a newspaper at hand, at a time when
the country is being besieged by fascism of the Left and of
the Right."

Beautiful words. Now I understand (or perhaps understood
then too) that we were aspiring toward a microclimate, creating a microclimate so as to avoid the decision suggested by
so many friends, especially to me: Leave the country. Up to
the last day, the day of my kidnapping, which was subsequently converted into an arrest, we persisted in this battle,
and I refused to leave the country. In reply to an Israeli
friend who begged me to leave, I sent a brief note which he
later showed me on my arrival in Tel Aviv. It wound up by
saying: "I am one who belongs to Masada." How I would have
liked to remember that remark during torture sessions.

Is it any easier now to understand? What is perhaps still
lacking is the unifying link between Arlt's seven madmen

and Borges's definition of the Argentine. But let us turn our thoughts to that wide range of terrorist groups who have killed one another, killed their enemies of other political stripes as well as adversaries within their own party: Perónists assassinating Perónists, the military assassinating the military, union members assassinating union members, students other students, policemen other policemen. And let us also consider those vast para-police or paramilitary terrorist organizations that required arms, munitions, training camps, transport, ideological training, identity documents, clandestine prisons, dwellings, maintenance, all of whose funds emanated from the same source: kidnapping and blackmail, booty and plundering. Large ransoms were paid by kidnapped industrialists or executives (the highest in history was $60 million, obtained by leftist Perónist terrorists in the Born brothers kidnapping); monthly sums were paid by companies to right-wing and left-wing organizations simultaneously to assure that their executives wouldn't be assassinated or kidnapped; property, jewelry, and works of art were "confiscated" when an arrest or kidnapping took place. Doesn't this recall The Astrologer's proposal: an ideology financed by the exploitation of brothels?

But does it, in the end, explain either present-day Argentina or the Argentina of the last decade? To my mind it does not, for there still remain innumerable details, both tragic and ridiculous, of assassinations, organized or improvised, spontaneous or premeditated, prompted by personal motives cloaked in ideological terms, or merely by terrorist sensuality. Hannah Arendt referred to Naziism as "the banality of evil." The extreme Left and extreme Right reached Argentina via the same criminal route, devoid of German precision but spiced with Latin American eroticism. Eduardo Galeano, a Uruguayan writer of the Left, wrote about one of his terrorist characters (admiringly, of course) as follows: "The first time in violence is like the first time in love." The book is called *Vagamundo (Vagabond)*.

Nonetheless, this mechanism of terror and violence still

remains unclear. And it must be portrayed in its total dimensions, for it has reached such magnitude that it cannot be understood simply in political, cultural, or electoral terms. Nor does the old struggle of democracy against extremism of the Right and the Left aptly define the Argentine situation. It may be simpler and more terrible than anything hitherto known by our generation in Latin America. It is a struggle between civilization and barbarism within a country of 25 million inhabitants toward the end of the twentieth century. And this barbarism—whether it be private or governmental, civil or military—must obviously be eradicated before it is possible to enter civilization. The political question in Argentina remains in abeyance until that moment when the country is in a position to enter civilization.

During my journalistic career, particularly as publisher and editor of *La Opinión,* I received countless threats. One morning two letters arrived in the same mail: one was from the rightist terrorist organization (protected and utilized by paramilitary groups), condemning me to death because of its belief that my militancy on behalf of the right to trial for anyone arrested and my battle for human rights were hindrances in overthrowing communism; the other letter was from the terrorist Trotskyite group, *Ejército Revolucionario Popular* (ERP)—the Popular Revolutionary Army—and indicated that if I continued accusing leftist revolutionaries of being Fascists and referring to them as the lunatic Left, I would be tried and most likely sentenced to death.

In the past I had never answered similar threats, but the incident struck me as so brutal and comical, so tragic and banal, that I wrote a few lines on page one of *La Opinión* in reply. I didn't say much, merely that we would continue to maintain our standards (a statement reiterated by so many newspapers and journalists all over the world that by now it has become tedious), and that I felt genuinely curious to know who would wind up with my corpse—the terrorists of the Left or those of the Right.

After all, it was a question of only one corpse, and the joke was irrelevant. One more dead journalist in a country where one hundred journalists had disappeared within the space of a few years was of no great significance. But the incident is useful in delving further into the Argentine drama: Can the community alone, without outside intervention, prevent either of the two fascisms from winding up with Argentina's corpse? Or if it cannot accomplish this on its own, then is collaboration possible among the international community to prevent either of them from doing so, and to enable Argentina's reincorporation into civilized society, into the contemporary civilization it abandoned fifty years ago?

3

When I founded *La Opinión*, I had been a political journalist
for newspapers, magazines, radio, and television for twenty-
four years. The first issue of the newspaper appeared on May
4, 1971, and I was arrested in April 1977. During that interval
in Argentina, six presidents governed—so to speak. Sanctions
against *La Opinión* took place under all these regimes in the
form of judicial *de facto* measures, bomb assaults at my home
and office, the murder or disappearance of one of my journalists, and finally my arrest and the army's confiscation of the
newspaper. The most subtle form of sanction was economic,
for Argentina—though this is not commonly known—is a
country whose economy is almost seventy percent govern-
ment-controlled, and advertising from government agencies
constitutes a decisive portion of the revenue a newspaper
requires to ensure its financial solvency. Successive adminis-
trations suspended government advertising in *La Opinión*
whenever an article provoked them. One government invented a Machiavellian stratagem: It induced the association
of newspaper distributors, which it controlled, to request a
larger number of copies of *La Opinión* than the market
could absorb. In the event the newspaper refused, the distributors were released from their distribution agreement

with it; if the newspaper complied, delivering this inordinate quantity of unneeded newspapers resulted in excessive production costs. Whenever such economic sanctions took place, *La Opinión* turned to its readers, increasing its price until it became the most expensive newspaper in the country, but one that remained, unlike the others, independent of public or private advertising.

La Opinión, curiously enough, was a moderate newspaper. It was often compared to *Le Monde,* but in relation to the ideological position of the French daily, one could say that *La Opinión* was a typically liberal newspaper. Every day it committed what in Argentina was construed as a capital sin: it used precise language to describe actual situations so that its articles were comprehensible and direct. Might one claim that *La Opinión* was attacked for semantic reasons? Not so, though semantics is the method employed in Argentina to avoid seeing problems in their total dimensions. Newspapers write virtually in code, resorting to euphemisms and circumlocutions, speaking in a roundabout way, as do leaders, politicians, and intellectuals. One might have the impression that Argentina is a rich heir dissipating its inherited fortune—in this instance, the wealth derived from the generations that ruled between 1860 and 1930—but is trying as hard as possible to conceal the fact that the fortune is dwindling and nobody is making any effort to restore it. In this sense, *La Opinión* was genuinely provocative. On more than one occasion it published news stories that had appeared in other papers but were completely incomprehensible to those outside the informed inner circle, and explained these articles so that the average reader could understand them. Actually, it was an explanation of a news item that had appeared five days before in a provincial paper, without measures having been taken against that paper, that led to President Isabel Perón's ten-day suspension of *La Opinión.* Similarly, President Videla suspended *La Opinión* for three days for having published an explanation of an article that had appeared in a Jesuit magazine, although that particular issue of the Catholic journal was not even confiscated.

The Argentine rulers wanted to be viewed like Dorian Gray, but *La Opinión* was the mirror hidden above, which appeared daily on the streets, presenting Dorian Gray's true face.

The semantics of the three governing factions that rule Argentina—the Perónists, trade unions, and armed forces—constitutes one of the oddest processes in political practice. In essence, this is not unprecedented, considering the accumulated experience of fascism and communism with propaganda, slogans, and the structuring of a reality contradictory every step of the way to actual events. But fascism and communism are political phenomena of great magnitude and encompass nations of vast geopolitical and international interests. The semantic process of these ideologies tends to create not only an inner reality within its own territories but also an agile and flexible instrument for international penetration. But why should such a phenomenon occur in a country that is relatively small, practically devoid of demographic or economic growth, containing 25 million inhabitants on 3 million square kilometers who could live peacefully off its existing wealth and enjoy greater ease than even the Swiss?

During a meeting of the International Monetary Fund, a Brazilian economist who I'm sure prefers to remain anonymous defined the different economic groupings in the world as follows: (1) the developed countries; (2) the undeveloped countries; (3) Japan, which occupies a category of its own, inasmuch as these small islands, despite their lack of natural resources and raw materials, have become an industrial power with a permanent demographic boom; and (4) Argentina, because the Japanese work and save for years in order to be able to live one day like the Argentines, who neither work nor save.

Juan Domingo Perón used to say that "Violence from above engenders violence from below"—a statement that could be found in any Harvard, MIT, or Hudson Institute study on the aggressive feelings of populations with meager resources. A liberal statement, a sociological equation, which in an organized country might lead merely to a polemic on the ways in which such aggressiveness can be eliminated through housing, education, or public health programs. In Argentina, however, Perónist youth understood at once what Perón was saying: he approved of violence and terrorism, and would lend his support to any murder, kidnapping, or assault that fit into his goals for the conquest or reconquest of power.

Another statement epitomizing an important political clue to the last ten years in Argentina was taken by Perón from Pericles: "Everything according to measure, and yet in harmony." I found this same phrase in an article by Nahum Goldman that was published in *La Opinión*. A serene saying, tranquil-sounding, not hard to understand and appreciate, it justifies a political process meticulously carried out so as to produce the smallest possible number of critical situations. But Perónists, and all Argentines, understood immediately what it signified: anyone opposed to the tactical methods established by Perón would be executed by the boys, pushed from below by the violence from above. Those boys who, logically, regarded Pericles' statement as a kind of revolutionary strategy no different from Fidel Castro's phase in the Sierra Maestra or Mao Zedong's in the Yenan Mountains. "Measure" referred to Perón's orders, and "in harmony" to the machine gun.

Another of Perón's statements in his infinite semantic creativity was "Reality is the only truth." This might be construed as an incitement to careful, meticulous scrutiny of data culled from reality in order to discover peaceful, moderate paths toward a political solution. In practice, however, it formed the basis for Perónist intolerance of any solution outside the ken of its own followers, schemes, or totalitarian rigidity, and the justification of utterly irrational acts in the economic, cultural, and political spheres. In fact, the only admissible reality was Perónism, since that was the majority, and the only truth was the Perónist way of life.

The form of combat devised by the other political parties was also a semantic process: to negotiate without contradicting, to await the inevitable crisis and deterioration of officialdom rather than exert any opposition that might induce a crisis which could explode like a grenade in Argentina's face. The anti-Perónist newspapers employed euphemisms to present their criticism, euphemisms that were comprehensible to the parties involved in the game but not to the readers. *La Opinión*, however, was attempting (or perhaps flirting daily with) suicide to expose the true face of Dorian Gray.

A similar instance occurred with the military government following the defeat of Perónism. The revolt against the Perón presidency found its principal proponent in *La Opinión,* for we insisted on the need to fill the vacuum in which the country dwelt. Military leaders were prepared, according to long conversations between them and editors of *La Opinión,* for a revolution to take place in order to terminate the violence of both Left and Right, to enforce sanctions against corruption, to curb terrorism through legal channels, and to overcome the danger of super-inflation. The whole nation longed for peace. During Isabel Perón's last year of rule, *La Opinión* voiced these principles day after day; and finally in March 1976, when the army seized the government, the entire country, including the Perónists, breathed a sigh of relief.

But once again semantics ran parallel to a reality that daily contradicted it. General Videla's government strove to accomplish peaceful acts; it spoke of peace and understanding, maintaining that the revolution was not aimed against anyone in particular or any special sector. But military leaders hastily organized their personal domains, each one becoming a warlord in the zone under his control, whereupon the chaotic, anarchistic, irrational terrorism of the Left and of Fascist death squads gave way to intrinsic, systemized, rationally planned terrorism. Each officer of a military region had his own prisoners, prisons, and form of justice, and even the central power was unable to request the freedom of an individual when importuned by international pressure. Every individual whose freedom was solicited in the years 1976–78 by the central power, the Catholic Church, or some international organization immediately "disappeared." It was usually necessary to track down the individual in question in a clandestine prison and then submit a petition indicating the hour, day, and place that he'd been seen alive.

Whenever the government was forced to admit repressive excesses, the wording of its self-criticism tended to suggest merely that a certain ward of prisoners had gone one night without food. Whenever a military officer referred to those who'd "gone away forever," it sounded rather like a melancholy remark intended to recall those who'd emigrated to distant lands and continents to rebuild their lives. The semantic process could acquire even sudden clownish overtones. When Thomas Reston, a spokesman for the U.S. State Department, expressed his government's concern over attacks on the headquarters of certain organizations that defended human rights in Argentina, the reply given by one of the ministers indicated that the Argentine government was likewise concerned and, at the same time, wished to protest the existence of the Ku Klux Klan in the United States. Newspaper, radio, and television commentators reinforced this attitude. How to explain that the Ku Klux Klan did not form part of the North American government and occupied no seat in President Carter's cabinet, whereas in Argentina the moderates of the military revolution had thus far been unable to gain control over repression or over, in many instances, the official operation of parallel justice from their local versions of the Ku Klux Klan.

If *La Opinión* succeeded in surviving between March 1976 and April 1977, the first year of military government, it was because army moderates decided that this journal, critical but not antagonistic, opposed to terrorism but supportive of human rights, ought to survive. The continued existence of *La Opinión* was a credit abroad; it backed the philosophy of future national reconstruction, it upheld the thesis of national unity, and was committed on a daily basis to curbing extremist excesses. The moderates, in those early years, comprised a minority in the armed forces, and only their political acumen enabled them to retain a foothold in the ongoing process. Political parties, virtually all civil institutions, the Catholic Church, and Western governments maintaining the most satisfactory relations with Argentina all calculated that the best strategy was patience—to wait for time to pass and the extremists to weaken, and in the meantime not to impose excessive demands on the moderates.

On paper, this approach was not implausible. Elections seemed inevitable. But in my position as editor-in-chief of *La Opinión,* every day I had to confront that distinction between extremists and moderates when relatives of those who had disappeared would show up and assume that *La Opinión* could assist in finding them. More than once I had to explain that an article in *La Opinión* could mean a death sentence; nonetheless, their loneliness and the dearth of news made them believe that printing an article on a disappearance was advantageous. At least it fortified them in their solitude and for the upcoming struggle. On balance, I'm unable to weigh the results. I know that I saved the lives of some, and believe others were killed merely because *La Opinión* demanded knowledge of their whereabouts. But in the long run the battle, it seems to me, had to be fought, so that at least there *was* a battle, embryonic as it might be. Some people hold that the only possible response to totalitarian repression—whether Fascist or Communist—is to go underground or into exile. Both of these solutions were contrary to my philosophy. I thought it necessary at the time to go one step further: to attack the leaders of extremist military groups directly. It may have been one such group, unbeknownst to President Videla and the central government, that kidnapped me.

How was one, then, to judge the moderates? They were, are, and will always be opposed to all excesses. Yet they opposed none of these. Was this due to lack of strength? They

simply said they were allowing the unavoidable to occur. I
recall a remark made by the chief of the Army General Staff
to a diplomat who intervened on my behalf when I was
arrested: "Timerman isn't delinquent, but it's best not to
meddle in the affair. Don't get involved." Hence support of
the moderates, acknowledging their immobility and the
enormity of extremist excesses, constituted a veritable leap
into a vacuum. This attitude elsewhere had provided Hitler
with a free hand for seizing power in Germany and had
empowered the Communists in Cuba to take over the youthful, romantic revolution of the Sierra Maestra against Ful-
gencio Batista's dictatorship.

The moderates, in my opinion, had to be supported by way
of public pressure rather than patience. The Western governments did not view the situation similarly, nor did the
Church, the Argentine political parties, or other Argentine
newspapers. Nonetheless the fact that this impunity was at
least disputed has gone on record. At present it's hard to
determine the significance of the policy of *La Opinión,* although this will certainly be clearer in the future when we
have a better perspective.

One might say that my present freedom is a result of the
patience exercised by the moderates. My own belief is that
the concessions made on my behalf by the moderates toward
the extremists have been harmful to Argentina on an international scale, for the case should have impelled the moderates to wage a more militant battle against the extremists,
particularly since they would have been joined in that battle
by an army minority plus a popular majority, political parties,
and civil institutions. I believe the moderates would have
won the battle, and Argentina would have been saved some
years of tragedy.

I was kidnapped by the extremist sector of the army. From
the outset, President Rafael Videla and General Roberto
Viola tried to convert my disappearance into an arrest in
order to save my life. They did not succeed. My life was
spared because this extremist sector was also the heart of

Nazi operations in Argentina. From the very first interrogation, they figured they had found what they'd been looking for for so long: one of the sages of Zion, a central axis of the Jewish anti-Argentine conspiracy.

Question: Are you Jewish?
Answer: Yes.
Question: Are you a Zionist?
Answer: Yes.
Question: Is *La Opinión* Zionist?
Answer: *La Opinión* supports Zionism since it is the liberation movement of the Jewish people. It considers Zionism to be a movement of high positive values, the study of which can shed light on many problems related to building national Argentine unity.
Question: Then it *is* a Zionist newspaper?
Answer: If you wish to put it in those terms, yes.
Question: Do you travel to Israel often?
Answer: Yes.
Question: Do you know the Israeli ambassador?
Answer: Yes.

My first interrogation took place after I'd been standing for several hours with my arms handcuffed behind my back, my eyes blindfolded. It was a sort of revelation for the interrogators. Why kill the hen that lays the golden eggs? Better to exploit him for the most important trial against the international Jewish conspiracy.

That's what saved my life. From that moment on, my arrest was officially recognized. The moderates tried for two years to get me released, and even thirty months later, when my freedom had been obtained, it was exploited as a pretext by the extremists to attempt a revolution to expel the moderates from power. A revolution that concluded in a ridiculous farce in the city of Córdoba—a forty-eight-hour uprising with no fighting, no bloodshed, only surrender.

Seen in this light, one could say that the moderates were correct. I think they were not. They could have combated the extremists much sooner; they had, and in fact still have, greater strength than they imagine, and thousands of lives might have been saved. On the other hand, it's hard to talk about tactics when countless innocent people lost their lives.

My life was saved because the Nazis were overly Nazi; because they believed, as they informed me, that World War III had begun and that they enjoyed every conceivable impunity. One of the interrogators, known as Captain Beto, told me: "Only God gives and takes life. But God is busy elsewhere, and we're the ones who must undertake this task in Argentina."

4

The news was the main topic in my home as far back as my memory takes me. News in all its forms and stages. As a child, I listened to grown-ups talking about the pogroms of the Russian Civil War. At home, newspapers bringing the first news about Hitler were devoured, and, later on, with others of my generation, I followed the long path leading from the Spanish Civil War to the present day. Newspapers, novels, films, poetry, war diaries, political works, the memoirs of those who had escaped the prison camps of Franco, Pétain, Mussolini, Hitler, Stalin; books about repression in Cuba, Nicaragua, Paraguay, Vietnam, China; interrogations in jails all over Africa—countless battles, countless tortures, countless blows, countless killers. One might logically assume that I thought I knew it all, knew what a political prisoner was, how he suffered in jail, the things a tortured man felt. But I knew nothing. And it's impossible to convey what I know now.

In the long months of confinement, I often thought of how to transmit the pain that a tortured person undergoes. And always I concluded that it was impossible.

It is a pain without points of reference, revelatory symbols, or clues to serve as indicators.

CELL WITHOUT A NUMBER

A man is shunted so quickly from one world to another that he's unable to tap a reserve of energy so as to confront this unbridled violence. That is the first phase of torture: to take a man by surprise, without allowing him any reflex defense, even psychological. A man's hands are shackled behind him, his eyes blindfolded. No one says a word. Blows are showered upon a man. He's placed on the ground and someone counts to ten, but he's not killed. A man is then led to what may be a canvas bed, or a table, stripped, doused with water, tied to the ends of the bed or table, hands and legs outstretched. And the application of electric shocks begins. The amount of electricity transmitted by the electrodes—or whatever they're called—is regulated so that it merely hurts, or burns, or destroys. It's impossible to shout—you howl. At the onset of this long human howl, someone with soft hands supervises your heart, someone sticks his hand into your mouth and pulls your tongue out of it in order to prevent this man from choking. Someone places a piece of rubber in the man's mouth to prevent him from biting his tongue or destroying his lips. A brief pause. And then it starts all over again. With insults this time. A brief pause. And then questions. A brief pause. And then words of hope. A brief pause. And then insults. A brief pause. And then questions.

What does a man feel? The only thing that comes to mind is: They're ripping apart my flesh. But they didn't rip apart my flesh. Yes, I know that now. They didn't even leave marks. But I felt as if they were tearing my flesh. And what else? Nothing that I can think of. No other sensation? Not at that moment. But did they beat you? Yes, but it didn't hurt.

When electric shocks are applied, all that a man feels is that they're ripping apart his flesh. And he howls. Afterwards, he doesn't feel the blows. Nor does he feel them the next day, when there's no electricity but only blows. The man spends days confined in a cell without windows, without light, either seated or lying down. He also spends days tied to the foot of a ladder so that he's unable to stand up and can only kneel, sit, or stretch out. The man spends a month not being allowed to wash himself, transported on the floor of an automobile to various places for interrogation, fed badly, smelling bad. The man is left enclosed in a small cell for forty-eight hours, his eyes blindfolded, his hands tied behind him, hearing no voice, seeing no sign of life, having to perform his bodily functions upon himself.

And there is not much more. Objectively, nothing more.

Or perhaps there is much more. And I'm trying to forget it. Every day, since my release, I've been waiting for some vital shock to take place, some deep, extended nightmare to explode suddenly in the middle of the night, allowing me to relive it all—something that will take me back to the original scene, purify me, and then restore me to this place where I am now writing. But nothing has happened, and I find this calm terrifying.

A journalist asked me how freedom feels. I still do not feel it. I'm repressing the sensation of freedom because I fear that, otherwise, I may find myself relinquishing the profound marks imprinted on me, imprints that must be relieved in order to be relinquished.

Although I cannot transmit the magnitude of that pain, I can perhaps offer some advice to those who will suffer torture in the future. The human being will continue to be tortured in different countries, under different regimes. In the year and a half I spent under house arrest I devoted much thought to my attitude during torture sessions and during the period of solitary confinement. I realized that, instinctively, I'd developed an attitude of absolute passivity. Some fought against being carried to the torture tables; others begged not to be tortured; others insulted their torturers. I represented sheer passivity. Because my eyes were blindfolded, I was led by the hand. And I went. The silence was part of the terror. Yet I did not utter a word. I was told to undress. And I did so, passively. I was told, when I sat on a bed, to lie down. And, passively, I did so. This passivity, I believe, preserved a great deal of energy and left me with all my strength to withstand the torture. I felt I was becoming a vegetable, casting aside all logical emotions and sensations—fear, hatred, vengeance —for any emotion or sensation meant wasting useless energy.

In my opinion, this is sound advice. Once it's been determined that a human being is to be tortured, nothing can prevent that torture from taking place. And it's best to allow yourself to be led meekly toward pain and through pain, rather than to struggle resolutely as if you were a normal human being. The vegetable attitude can save a life.

I had a similar experience during those long days of solitary confinement. More than once I was brusquely awakened by someone shouting: "Think. Don't sleep, think." But I refused to think. I behaved as if my mind were occupied with infinite diverse tasks. Concrete, specific tasks, chores. To think meant becoming conscious of what was happening to me, imagining what might be happening to my wife and children; to think meant trying to work out how to relieve this situation, how to wedge an opening in my relationship with the jailers. In that solitary universe of the tortured, any attempt to relate to reality was an immense painful effort leading to nothing.

When my eyes were not blindfolded, I'd spend a few minutes—I believe it was minutes—moving a hand or a leg and observing the movement, fixedly, in order to experience some sense of mobility. Once a fly entered the cell, and it was a real holiday watching it flit around for hours, till it disappeared through the small crack by which the jailers communicated with me.

Then, after those "important" episodes in my life were over, my mental labor began. I decided to write a book about my wife's eyes. It would be entitled *Risha's Eyes in the Cell Without a Number.* Curiously, I wasn't thinking about my wife as such, for that would have been acutely painful, but was organizing myself, like a poet at his work table, before undertaking some inspired professional endeavor. I held a long discussion with myself about what style to employ. Modeling it after Pablo Neruda would be reiterative, an inadequate romanticism perhaps; whereupon I recalled Federico

García Lorca's style in "Poet in New York," and came up
with a few lines, but then began wondering if perhaps Stefan
George's symbolism might not be more appropriate, for in a
certain way it was linked with Franz Kafka's world. But if my
quest were to end here, that meant that my mental writing
had to begin. And the important thing was for that task to last
as long as possible. I recalled the work of Chaim Nachman
Bialik, particularly one of his poems about a pogrom, but his
work struck me as being too peculiar to eastern European
experience; as for Vladimir Mayakovsky, he seemed overly
Russian in his love poems to Lila Brick and too verbose in his
poetry about the Russian Revolution. I likewise dismissed
Paul Éluard; Claudel was unadaptable, and Aragon didn't
especially impress me. There remained, of course, the poets
of my youth: Walt Whitman, Carl Sandburg, and the Span-
iards Miguel Hernández and Luis Cernuda. Finally, I settled
on Stephen Spender, and began to write, in my mind.

One might think that the selection of style would bring
back memories of the times when I first read those writers.
Memory is the chief enemy of the solitary tortured man—
nothing is more dangerous at such moments. But I managed
to develop certain passivity-inducing devices for withstand-
ing torture and anti-memory devices for those long hours in
the solitary cell. I refused to remember anything that bore
on life experience—I was a professional stoic dedicated to his
task. The book I was working on absorbed me for days,
though now I can't remember a single line. For a time I
recalled paragraphs, but now they are profoundly buried.
And the thought that they may resurface is as frightening as
the notion of reliving those solitary hours. Some day I suppose I'll be forced to re-encounter myself by way of all that.
Perhaps I'm experiencing the same problem as Argentina, an
unwillingness to be aware of one's own drama.

Another activity of mine was to organize a bookstore. I
thought about how one day I'd be free, figuring that several
long years might elapse before that moment, maybe ten or
fifteen. Thinking in terms of a prolonged span of time is

extremely useful when there is no fixed sentence, for it an-
nihilates hope, and hope is synonymous with anxiety and
anguish. I imagined my eventual arrival in Israel and the
need to organize some work. I decided that a bookstore
would be the most suitable way for two voracious readers like
myself and my wife to earn a living. I speculated on all the
details: the size of the main room, the name, the typography
of the letters printed on the windows, the type of books we'd
sell, whether it would be a good idea to install a literary salon
on an upper floor or perhaps an experimental film society. A
detailed task of this sort could easily keep me occupied for
days. Following the same method, I organized a newspaper
in Madrid, another in New York, my life on a kibbutz, and
a film by Ingmar Bergman on the solitude of a tortured man.

Long afterwards, I realized that I had developed a with-
drawal technique. I tried through every available means,
while inside my solitary cell, during interrogations, long torture sessions, and after sessions, when only time remained, all
of time, time on all sides and in every cranny of the cell, time
suspended on the walls, on the ground, in my hands, only
time, I tried to maintain some professional activity, discon-
nected from the events around me or that I imagined to be
going on around me. Deliberately, I evaded conjecture on
my own destiny, that of my family and the nation. I devoted
myself simply to being consciously a solitary man entrusted
with a specific task.

At times, something in the mechanism would fail, and I
had to devote several hours to reconstructing it: some lingering physical pain following an interrogation, hunger, the
need for a human voice, for contact, for a memory. Yet I
always managed to reconstruct the mechanism of with-
drawal, and thus was able to avoid lapsing into that other
mechanism of tortured solitary prisoners which leads them
to establish a bond with their jailer or torturer. Both parties
seem to feel some need of the other: for the torturer, it is a
sense of omnipotence, without which he'd find it hard perhaps to exercise his profession—the torturer needs to be

needed by the tortured; whereas the man who's tortured finds in his torturer a human voice, a dialogue for his situation, some partial exercise of his human condition—he asks for pity, to go to the bathroom, for another plate of soup, he asks for the result of a football game.

I was able to avoid all of that.

Following my transfer to a legal cell and permission for family visits, the guards would have allowed packages of food to be brought to me in exchange for a gift. I didn't take advantage of this system, and my wife was told by a policeman that I was punishing myself, playing the martyr. I don't know why I opted for such proud asceticism. Now, I am unable to judge how sensible an idea this was, though at that point it helped to instill an idea of my own reserves, and I rejoiced. The other recourse would have provided consolation, but not joy.

After the War Council's ruling that no charges existed against me and that a trial would not be held, I remained imprisoned for another two years, although my situation in legal imprisonment improved. There were other prisoners, we were allowed to talk, the cells were open and each was provided with a latrine (a hole in the ground). We could bathe every day, we began cooking our own food, played long card games, read newspapers, and were allowed to receive certain books, clean clothing, blankets and sheets, a radio. We'd all been tortured, to a greater or lesser degree. From our dialogues, we discovered that a torture session to soften a man up always followed immediately upon his arrest, though in some cases many days elapsed between torture session and interrogation. Other prisoners were never even interrogated.

Inevitably, since my release, the first question I'm asked concerns the torture I underwent. Yet, for the man who's been tortured and has survived, this is perhaps the least important topic. In conversations with other prisoners, I discovered the following curious fact: our preoccupations revolved around how long we'd be in jail, our family's situation and economic needs; and if by chance the topic of torture came up, it was only via a random remark that didn't seem of consummate interest to anyone. "I had five days on the machine." "They put me on the machine with my clothes on." "The machine hurt my head." Sometimes, on hearing the howls that rose from the basement, a prisoner might say, as if in passing, "They're giving someone the machine."

The victim, following his torture and during the waiting period—whether he's been sentenced or is ignorant of his fate—devotes himself to the daily needs of life. Torture forms part of an ordinary routine, something already undergone and now the turn of others—some of whom will survive, others not. It occupies a very limited place in the life of the tortured person, and when he's newly freed and able to speak openly and be openly questioned, he's astonished at the importance mankind attaches to the subject.

The soldiers who tortured me were so proud of finally having laid hands on me that they strove to spread the details of that great event, and even embellished it, I believe, with nonexistent details. They spoke of the mirrored rooms where the electric shocks were applied and of the numerous observers who witnessed the episode from the other side. I think the tortures were performed in old buildings, disguised as commissaries, in small villages near Buenos Aires, generally some rebuilt kitchen or a large cell where an electric cable could be installed. Torture centers existed, of course, in military barracks, but always in basements or abandoned kitchens.

The torturers, nevertheless, try to create a more sophisticated image of the torture sites, as if thereby endowing their activity with a more elevated status. Their military leaders encourage this fantasy; and the notion of important sites, exclusive methods, original techniques, novel equipment, allows them to present a touch of distinction and legitimacy to the world.

This conversion of dirty, dark, gloomy places into a universe of spontaneous innovation and institutional "beauty" is one of the most arousing pleasures for torturers. It is as if they felt themselves to be masters of the force required to alter reality. And it places them again in the world of omnipotence. This omnipotence in turn they feel assures them of impunity—a sense of immunity to pain, guilt, emotional imbalance.

I'm seated on a chair in the yard. Hands tied behind my back. Eyes blindfolded. It's drizzling, and I'm soaked. I keep moving my head and legs in an effort to keep warm. I've peed, the pee has turned icy, and the skin on my legs, where the urine ran down, hurts. I hear some steps, and a voice asks me if I'm cold. I'm untied from the chair and led into a warm room. I was brought to this clandestine prison today. Taken from central federal police headquarters in the city of Buenos Aires. I later learned that a prisoner who saw me leave asked the head of our ward for permission to inform my family that he'd seen me, arms tied behind my back, go peacefully without offering resistance. He was told that it wasn't advisable to get involved, inasmuch as I'd been removed without a written order or record of transfer, which meant that I was going to be executed.

It is hot. They seat me on a chair and take the blindfold off my eyes. It's handed to me. We're in a spacious kitchen. Before me are some smiling men, big and fat, dressed in civilian clothing.

Weapons are everywhere. The men are drinking coffee, and one of them offers me some in a tin cup. He keeps smiling. Tells me to sip it slowly, asks if I want a blanket, invites me to come close to the stove, to eat something.

Everything about him transmits generosity, a desire to protect me. He asks if I'd like to lie down a while on the bed. I tell him no. He tells me there are some female prisoners on the grounds, if I'd care to go to bed with one of them. I tell him no. This gets him angry because he wants to help me and, by not allowing him to, I upset his plan, his aim.

In some way he needs to demonstrate to me and to himself his capacity to grant things, to alter my world, my situation. To demonstrate to me that I need things that are inaccessible to me and which only he can provide.

I've noticed this mechanism repeated countless times.

One feels tempted to combat this tendency on the part of the torturers, to confront it as almost a unique possibility for feeling oneself to be alive; yet such futile battles lead to nought. It's best to acknowledge and accept the torturers' omnipotence in such unimportant matters. Many times you reject them more out of your own omnipotence than out of a competitive spirit toward the torturer or a lucid decision to put up a fight, though it's definitively a gratuitous act of pride.

Out of weariness, perhaps, or resignation, or that sensation which so often assails the tortured—a presentiment of imminent death—I do not answer. He insults me but doesn't strike me. Again he puts the blindfold on my eyes. Takes my hand and leads me out of the kitchen. Seats me on the chair and ties my hands behind me.

It continues to drizzle.

The man sighs and goes off, casting toward me, I suppose, a final glance of incomprehension.

5

In the entrance hall of *La Opinión* stands a weeping mother asking to see me. I don't have the strength for this meeting because I'm as despairing as she. My secretary persuades the woman to give her reason for coming to see me. Her two children have disappeared. They were taken from the house while she was out. A girl and a boy, eighteen and fifteen years old. The neighbors said they saw two cars with armed men. She was told at her district police station that they had no knowledge of the incident, that it was not an official act. She's convinced that the editor-in-chief of a newspaper is sufficiently powerful to find her children.

It's a lie. She isn't convinced, for she knows that I can do nothing. Everyone knows I can do nothing. But they've no place to go, and come to *La Opinión* because they claim it's the only daily newspaper concerned about the disappeared. The majority are unaware of the existence of any other paper which on a daily basis bids the government respect the laws and at least publish a list of those who've been arrested. The Buenos Aires *Herald* is in English, and my visitors do not read English.

I could anticipate this woman's story and therefore didn't receive her. I receive some, others not. It depends on the degree of despair that I'm feeling the day they arrive. And they arrive in large numbers. How can I tell this woman that if I published the story about her children, it would most likely amount to a death sentence? How can I tell her that the government will never tolerate the assumption that a newspaper article can save a life? To permit this would mean losing the power of repression, the utilization of Fear and Silence.

Yet when my secretary tells me the story, how can I live with that?

Well, one can live with it. The Germans did, the Italians did, the Russians do, the Paraguayans do, the Chileans do, the Czechs do, the Uruguayans do.

Between 1966 and 1973 there are three military governments in Argentina, presided over by three generals. The entire institutional scheme is organized under the pompous heading of the Argentine Revolution. It begins with great optimism, but after 1969 finds itself on a dead-end street due to widespread resistance to the economic, social, and political situation. During this period Perónism begins to ally itself with all the other political parties in demanding that elections be called, and simultaneously starts organizing the Special Formations of urban guerrillas known as the Montoneros. Juan Domingo Perón calls them Special Formations because he doesn't want to lend official support to Perónist guerrillas and thereby be accused of subversion.

The military dictatorship enters a crisis due to its inability to devise a suitable political formula to deal with the situation, and elections are called. All the political parties, newspapers, and institutions support this solution. Perónism triumphs by a wide margin, but with a candidate, Hector Campora, who is basically supported—and dominated—by the leftist and Montonero sectors of Perónism. A couple of months later the situation is again untenable, and Juan Domingo Perón organizes a denunciation of the individual who'd been his candidate because the army has vetoed him as a potential president. He denounces Campora, new elections have to be called, and no one this time can veto Perón. Besides, the nation longs for Perón, assuming that he has sufficient authority to end the violence.

By this time, Perón's right wing has developed its own subversive activity through the Triple A (American Anticommunist Alliance), headed by José López Rega, Perón's private secretary for several years.

The Montoneros assassinate those engaged in their suppression; those who they believe are so engaged; those whom they regard as doing nothing to oppose those who suppress them; those who speak up against violence of both the Right and the Left because of their belief that members of the violent Left are accomplices of the Right; second-rank politicians who are friends of first-rank politicians who refuse to make deals with the Montoneros; politicians who they imagine might at some point interfere with their future plans because these politicians are liberals and would attract leftist youth; and leftist journalists who are opposed to violence and hence plant confusion in the minds of Montonero guerrilla fighters. The Montoneros engage in kidnapping as well, considering it logical that men who are able to afford a ransom should return to society their ill-gotten gains.

The Triple A engages in killing Montoneros, or those they assume to be Montoneros; they murder liberal politicians because their demands for legal trials of arrested Montoneros are regarded as a form of complicity with the Left; they murder defense lawyers of arrested Montoneros, regarding them as a branch of the guerrilla force; and they murder writers and leftist journalists, even though the latter may be anti-guerrilla, because their denunciations of right-wing terrorism are regarded as weakening the repressive will of Argentine society. The Triple A obtains its funds for salaries and the purchase of weapons and automobiles, and for its clandestine prisons, from the sale of booty acquired in raids and the ransom paid for kidnapped individuals—these generally being financially powerful members of the Jewish community.

The Montoneros succeed in forcing five hundred large business firms to pay a monthly protection sum against kidnapping or assault of their executives. The Triple A obtains a copy of this list and forces these five hundred large firms to subscribe to its financial support. The companies thus pay both organizations.

(On assuming power in 1976, the army incorporates into its operational structures the entire Triple A framework, with the exception of its leader, José López Rega, who is out of the country, but not sought out. They also get hold of the list of the five hundred firms and negotiate a substantial contribution from them for the fight against subversion. Again the companies pay.)

The ranks of the Triple A are made up of policemen and retired noncommissioned officers, usually those who've had disciplinary problems, committed some crime, or been punished for other offenses while in the ranks. The climate of violence envelops the entire nation. It is still assumed that Juan Domingo Perón can resolve the situation, and his margin of victory is even greater than that obtained by Campora. Despite being burdened in the election slate by the dead weight of his wife, he wins by almost seventy percent of the vote. He is now the third Perónist president in 1973. He cannot, however, quell the violence, and it's hard to tell whether he actually wishes to do so. A year later he is dead, and the situation starts to deteriorate further on every level, especially in terms of the economy and violence. His widow, Isabel Perón, manages to remain until March 1976, when the armed forces take power. Her twenty-month survival in office is not the result of her political acumen. The military, according to some observers, required that amount of time to lay their plans. In fact, the plans were already laid. The military needed something that proved to be of much greater importance: for the situation to deteriorate sufficiently so that the populace—press, political parties, Church, civil institutions—would regard military repression as inevitable. They needed allies who could be converted into accomplices. They needed the presence of such fear—about one's personal security, the economic crisis, the unknown—that it would provide them the margin of time and planning, and the needed passivity, to develop what they regarded as the only solution to leftist terrorism: extermination.

In Buenos Aires there's a place that we habitués had converted into an almost private club—the basement bar and restaurant of the Plaza Hotel. The wood paneling, tables, chairs, china, décor, all had a pleasantly Art Nouveau look. The tourists didn't bother us, they passed unnoticed. We were a sizable group, almost a crowd, of executives, businessmen, journalists, politicians, and high public officials.

We had our favorite dishes, enjoying that snobbism whereby maître d's, waiters, and sommeliers knew our tastes, and we knew them by name. We were all aware that whenever a table was reserved in advance, the secret service placed microphones to record our conversations, and this struck us as funny.

For years I held conversations in that place with future Argentine presidents as well as ex-presidents, with ministers and ex-ministers. I'd been practicing political journalism since 1946, and had come to that restaurant the first time as the guest of a politician. Now, head of a newspaper, I was the one who did the inviting.

Greetings were exchanged from table to table. I often saw high government officials greeting, in turn, civilians and military who were conspiring to overthrow that particular government. Sometimes people having lunch at one table wound up having coffee and liqueur with members of another table.

Diplomats came to ask questions, politicians to get information, journalists to gather news, the military to make contacts, corporate managers to do public relations with the present or future power.

That near-frivolous climate lasted for years, based on some

of those slogans Argentines like to quote of themselves: "God is Argentine. Nothing will happen here." "As long as bulls don't turn homosexual, the Argentine economy will flourish." But with the growth of rightist and leftist violence, the climate was changing. Our group began suffering some temporary casualties due to kidnappings and permanent casualties due to assassinations. We also missed those who had decided to live abroad. "Abroad" generally meant merely taking up residence in the beautiful beach resort of Punta del Este on the Uruguayan coast, barely forty minutes away by plane. We'd see them then on weekends or in the summer. But the fact is that during those years of 1972 through 1976, the participants began experiencing certain uncustomary worries and fears. Argentine reality ceased to have that air of gratuitous generosity, and we were overtaken by a constant uneasiness that we'd noticed among Europeans who had arrived in Buenos Aires shortly after World War II.

At one of these lunches, a few weeks after the fall of Isabel Perón, I met an officer of the Argentine navy. A common friend thought it necessary for us to speak to one another, and subsequently referred to our meeting as a dialogue between executioner and prospective suicide. It was assumed at that point, and I accepted it, that I was the suicide. Now, I'm not so sure.

Like many of the military of that period, he had an almost visceral hatred of the Perónist urban guerrillas. A political approach to the problem was hard for the military, even impossible, for on top of everything else their pride was wounded. The mere notion that the guerrillas wanted to beat them on the field of armed battle was more than they could tolerate. And though this was not the first time that the Argentine armed forces had taken power by overthrowing a popularly elected government, there had never been such systemized hatred. After all, the military had assumed power by dislodging elected governments in 1930, 1943, 1955, 1962,

1966, and now in 1976. This man, between forty and forty-five years of age, undoubtedly had begun his career at the age of thirteen in the Naval Academy and later joined the service, all those years witnessing his teachers, then his commanders, then himself, participate in the staging of military coups. And he himself could verify that never had such hatred existed in his ranks, nor such pleasure in the hatred.

All my efforts to steer the conversation toward an analysis of long- and short-term political measures that would benefit the country clashed with this conviction of the inevitable hatred and the need for extermination.

Barely forty-eight hours earlier, it had been discovered accidentally that the food destined for a group of officers in a military building had been poisoned. Had the lunch, which was canceled at the last minute, taken place, twelve high-ranking officials would certainly have died.

"What would you do, Timerman, if the culprits were arrested?"

"It was obviously the guerrillas. I'd submit them to military law and aim for a public trial, inviting journalists and foreign jurists to attend."

"For what purpose?"

"During the trial, the motives and methods of leftist subversion would inevitably emerge. Both the political hysteria of subversion and the dichotomy between their alleged aims and their methods would be clearly exposed. The whole muddle of improvised ideas that represents the guerrillas' pattern of thinking would be exposed, stripped of the romanticism given it by gossip, its clandestine nature and presumed martyrdom. Argentina, from an internal point of view, would benefit from such a political and judicial process, a political clarification that hasn't yet taken place. The political defeat of subversion is as important as its military defeat. Applying legal methods to repression eliminates one of the major elements exploited by subversion: the illegal nature of repression. As for the outside world, only legality can be acceptable to them. A government that adopts legal methods of repressing violence prevents the guerrillas from finding circumstantial allies among democratic men who are unable to accept the use of methods that inevitably recall those of Hitler, Stalin, or Idi Amin."

"But, Timerman, don't you understand that applying legal methods is equivalent to the death sentence? Those involved in the poisoning were soldiers. They're subject to the Code of Military Justice. They tried to kill their superiors. That's clear."

"I know. It's hard, but it's acceptable."

"So you'd be willing to accept the death sentence for those people?"

"Yes, I'd accept it. I do accept it."

"Fine. Well, you can be happy—they've already been executed."

"Without trial, defense, or anyone's knowledge?"

"Had we followed the method you advise, we would have had to delay their execution after they'd been sentenced to death."

"Why?"

"Because the Pope would have intervened."

"Possibly, but it's preferable to reject a petition from the Pope rather than mar the entire political process with a flagrant, bloody illegality that jeopardizes it in the future. All that you'd be accomplishing, once this phase is over, is a resurgence of vengeance and violence. The seeds of future violence are being planted."

"You're a Jew and don't understand that we can't deny a petition from the Holy Father."

"But the Pope would agree to a life sentence. . . ."

"And we'd be allowing a twenty-year-old terrorist to remain alive and maybe receive amnesty in ten to fifteen years when a Parliament in this country might pass amnesty laws. Imagine, he'd be only thirty or thirty-five, the age of a good military or political leader, with the added appeal of having been a martyr in his youth."

"That's why a political defeat is necessary, to create the

conditions for democratic coexistence, to enable the majority
of youth to seek their symbols elsewhere."

"But if we exterminate them all, there'll be fear for several
generations."

"What do you mean by all?"

"All . . . about twenty thousand people. And their relatives,
too—they must be eradicated—and also those who remember their names."

"And what makes you think that the Pope will not protest
such repression? Many governments, political leaders, trade
union leaders, and scientists throughout the world are already doing so. . . ."

"Not a trace or witness will remain."

"That's what Hitler attempted in his Night and Fog policy.
Sending to their death, reducing to ashes and smoke, those
he'd already stripped of any human trace or identity. Germany paid for each and every one of them. And is still paying,
with a nation that has remained divided."

"Hitler lost the war. We will win."

Entire families disappeared. The bodies were covered with
cement and thrown to the bottom of the river. The Plata
River, the Paraná River. Sometimes the cement was badly
applied, and corpses would wash up along the Argentine and
Uruguayan coasts. A mother recognized her fifteen-year-old
son, an Argentine, who appeared on the Uruguayan coast.
But that was an accident—the corpses usually vanished
forever.

The corpses were thrown into old cemeteries under existing graves. Never to be found.

The corpses were heaved into the middle of the sea from
helicopters.

The corpses were dismembered and burned.

Small children were turned over to grandparents when
there was mercy. Or presented to childless families. Or sold

to childless families. Or taken to Chile, Paraguay, Brazil, and given to childless families.

The people who participated in these procedures were generally transferred after a time to other regions or duties. The places where massacres took place were altered. Old buildings were demolished, their sites converted into public gardens or sold so that apartment houses could go up quickly. New buildings were converted to other uses.

Night and Fog.

Yet even amid victory the Argentine military discovered that everything was known. And that is the chief advantage they've handed the guerrillas and terrorism: an acknowledgment of terrorist irrationality as a policy, and the fact that their own irrationality exceeds that of their opponents.

The guerrillas responded with equal ferocity, though fewer resources, whereby everything was reduced to a confrontation of resources rather than a battle in which one political concept challenged another, one set of morals was pitted against another. The guerrilla force placed bombs in military lecture halls, in public dining rooms. But it could not compete. Yet in the ideological and moral realm it remained undefeated, and still wields the irrationality of repression, the abuse of power, the illegality of methods. That is its charter for the future.

No, there was no Night and Fog policy, nor will there be.

What there was, from the start, was the great silence, which appears in every civilized country that passively accepts the inevitability of violence, and then the fear that suddenly befalls it. That silence which can transform any nation into an accomplice.

That silence which existed in Germany, when even many well-intentioned individuals assumed that everything would return to normal once Hitler finished with the Communists and Jews. Or when the Russians assumed that everything would return to normal once Stalin eliminated the Trotskyites.

Initially, this was the conviction in Argentina. Then came fear. And after the fear, indifference. "Nothing happens to someone who stays out of politics."

Such silence begins in the channels of communication. Certain political leaders, institutions, and priests attempt to denounce what is happening, but are unable to establish contact with the population. The silence begins with a strong odor. People sniff the suicides, but it eludes them. Then silence finds another ally: solitude. People fear suicides as they fear madmen. And the person who wants to fight senses his solitude and is frightened.

Whereupon the silence reverts to patriotism. Fear finds its great moral revelation in patriotism, with its indubitable capacity for justification, its climate of glory and sacrifice. Only abroad, where there is neither Night nor Fog, are revelations formulated. That, however, is the Anti-Argentine Campaign.

It's best, therefore, to be a patriot and not remain solitary.

To stay out of politics and stay alive.

I leave the meeting at the Plaza Hotel filled with dreams of glory and combat. I accept the challenge, convinced that I hold many cards in my hand.

1. I send a journalist to London to spend a week at the Institute of Strategic Studies. I'm told that they've done several investigations on democratic methods of combating leftist terrorism. We collect material and publish a special supplement in *La Opinión.* I'm enthusiastic, and receive comments on the material from several military leaders. The British Embassy informs me that a number of military leaders have requested further information and want to consult the sources used by *La Opinión.* They send for some books. All the books concur, in varying degrees, that irrational, illegal repression compromises any future political victory and the formation of a democratic society. Illegal repression leaves the door open for a return of left-wing terrorism. Such

repression cannot be maintained indefinitely; when it is relaxed, terrorism returns, armed with a baggage of martyrdom.

2. I meet with an ex-president of Argentina—several of our ex-presidents are alive. I propose that they sign a joint document opposing violence in any form, of the Right or Left, in favor of legal methods of repression. Such a proposal might work, he thinks, if, in advance, a co-signed editorial expressing this principle were to appear in all the newspapers. I tell him I'm prepared to do this, and anticipate that certain small newspapers will join me, though it's unlikely that any other major paper will. But I'll try. Both of us fail. A member of his family dies in the attempt. A former secretary disappears forever.

3. There's a prestigious Catholic magazine that publishes analyses and commentaries of a positive, democratic nature and that upholds respect for the law and the legal process. The magazine comes out against certain repressive measures of the armed forces. I begin reproducing some of these articles in *La Opinión* to give them wider coverage. The editor of the magazine receives threats, and seems destined for transfer to a high position in the Vatican. The magazine continues, however, in its informative vein and makes no attempt to forbid my reproduction of its articles. I reprint another article from a Jesuit magazine. *La Opinión* is censured, and I'm informed that the author of the article, a priest, has been removed secretly from the country by the Jesuits out of fear for his life. I've a sense of being alone. I reproduce articles from small newspapers in the interior of the country. The papers are threatened and closed down. A bomb is thrown into the home of my editor on Catholic affairs. No one is killed.

4. I instruct political reporters and military columnists on *La Opinión* to broaden their contacts with leaders on both sides in order to locate any democratic leader who cares to comment or to write an article, any military official who

foresees the national peril in the illegality that is encroaching on the judicial process. Hardly any individuals care to talk to us. We are quite alone. Some reporters resign.

I'm thrown to the ground in the cell. It's hot. My eyes are blindfolded. The door opens and someone says that I'm to be moved. Two days have gone by without torture.

The doctor came to see me and removed the blindfold from my eyes. I asked him if he wasn't worried about my seeing his face. He acts surprised. "I'm your friend. The one who takes care of you when they apply the machine. Have you had something to eat?"

"I have trouble eating. I'm drinking water. They gave me an apple."

"You're doing the right thing. Eat lightly. After all, Gandhi survived on much less. If you need something, call me."

"My gums hurt. They applied the machine to my mouth."

He examines my gums and advises me not to worry, I'm in perfect health. He tells me he's proud of the way I withstood it all. Some people die on their torturers, without a decision having been made to kill them; this is regarded as a professional failure. He indicates that I was once a friend of his father's, also a police doctor. His features do seem familiar. I mention his father's name; this is indeed the son. He assures me that I'm not going to be killed. I tell him that I haven't been tortured for two days, and he's pleased.

Someone who's sent to fetch me cracks a joke: "To the gas chamber." The doctor gets angry. "We're not anti-Semites."

I'm transferred to Chief Police Headquarters in the city of La Plata. It takes half an hour to arrive, and as we enter the city my blindfold is removed and I'm allowed to sit up. Until now, I have been stretched out on the floor of the car. I recognize this city where I was a university student many years ago. A typical student city, with wide, tree-lined streets. I often came to Police Headquarters for various transactions. Now I'm led through the Fire Department entrance into the basement. I keep walking, my hands tied behind me. There's a corridor, and propped against one wall a high painter's ladder. The blindfold is again placed over my eyes, and one of my hands is tied to the bottom step of the ladder. I can either sit or lie down.

I remain this way for a couple of days, given only water. Every once in a while, I'm allowed to go to the bathroom. I'm spoken to amiably. Without shouts, insults, jeers, or sarcasm. People here recognize me, recall my television appearances. I'm told that the newspapers are writing about me, and I'm assured that I'll be all right.

My blindfold is removed—that is all. Different guards take turns. They alternate every six hours. I begin to recognize them. There's one who gives me a kick whenever he passes, without saying a word. I question another guard as to why he does this. He asks me to be understanding: The lad's a fine boy, but can't stand Jews, and that feeling is stronger than anything. In compensation, the man brings me a cup of coffee.

The interrogation takes place in the Chief Inspector's top-floor private dining room. Two people will question me; they're having lunch, and I'm invited to share their meal.

William Skardon, for over twenty years, was the chief examiner of Britain's internal security service, MI5. He interrogated the Russian atomic spy Klaus Fuchs, and obtained his confession. Skardon once reminisced on how an instructor had taught him the best method of interrogation: to repeat the same question many times, at different moments in the examination, as if it had never been asked before. The object is to verify how many changes the interrogated party introduces in his replies, then to point out to him the apparent contradictions, and keep insisting until the sought-after reply, or the one that is suspected to exist, is obtained.

That day, my interrogators' method is different. They assure me that all they want to do is hold a political conversation. They have certain points, however, in their favor: I've been subjected to long days of torture, while blindfolded, and have signed many papers which they claim are statements I made, and have also been forced to put my fingerprints on these papers. They flourish the papers in front of me, but don't allow me to read them. When an answer isn't to their liking, I'm immediately asked to tell them about my life. They scrutinize their papers. When I forget something, or begin at the age of fifteen, they tell me to start earlier, for example, at the time of my arrival in Argentina at five, or when I entered the Macabi Organization at eight.

If they like one of my answers, they have me write it out, sign it, and imprint it with the thumb of my right hand.

What arouses most enthusiasm are my theories on the need to combat both rightist and leftist terrorism. They anticipate using these ideas as the basis of their accusatory proceedings against me because "to identify legal forces with subversion is to be a subversive." I talk briefly about fascism of the Right and of the Left. They get furious, but don't strike me. It's a political conversation. How can I offend fascism by speaking of it in the same breath as the Left?

During this political conversation, which lasts for hours, perhaps fifteen or twenty, all the elements of my luncheon dialogue with the officer at the Plaza Hotel are repeated to some extent. But now, the exposition of my ideas is more a confession than an expression of a political proposal. My invocation of legality is distorted by the interrogators into a tactic designed to weaken the effectiveness of the security forces. My search for democratic allies amongst the political and military ranks is converted into a clandestine ploy to organize an instrument of opposition against the security forces. The reproduction of articles from other publications is converted into a satanic provocation intended to force the government to close down numerous publications, thereby confronting it with different sectors. Accepting the death penalty as the outcome of a trial is tantamount to presenting the armed forces as murderers.

I reiterate my ideas and convictions. And they're genuinely satisfied, for it provides the proof the security forces sought regarding the subversive nature of my journalistic activity. They ask if I'd like to have a bath, and suggest I take advantage of an opportunity I may not have again for some time. I hesitate slightly because of my great fatigue. I don't realize, they say, how bad I smell. Indeed, I haven't washed for almost a month. I accept the bath, with a guard posted at the door. In the mirror, I see how thin I am. I must have lost between twenty and twenty-five kilos, but there are no signs of torture evident on my body. The scent of soap and water . . . I discover them perhaps for the first time. I'm overwhelmed by a forgotten sensation, and am frightened, for until now I'd avoided memories as much as possible.

The examiner returns and asks about our persistent reporting on Russian dissidents. I reply that we began printing all the news we could get on the subject several years ago, and even engaged a Russian translator so that poems written by dissidents would at least have a direct rendition rather than one taken from the French or English. He tells me that I've failed to understand his question. He wants to know *why* we did it. I make one more effort to explain the ideology of *La Opinión*, the battle against leftist and rightist extremism, but he interrupts me. He's convinced that dissemination of dissident activity has as its only object the glorification of dissidence as a principle, and that transmission of that glorification to Argentine youth meant providing them with the ideological components of protest against the army.

He turns off the water faucet. I'm still covered with soap.

A strategy for helping that mother occurs to me. I realize that nothing can be printed in the newspaper, for it would be counterproductive; nor can I phone the garrison where the mother believes her children are being held, for then they'd be killed. What I can do, however, is to send a reporter to the headquarters of one of the three branches of the armed forces. Obviously, not the branch where the mother thinks they are held. And what is the point of this tactic?

Well, all that the reporter need do is to mention that an officer from the branch actually holding the children had made a remark to him indicating that both children were being incarcerated at the headquarters presently being visited. And that he'd heard this same remark from various political leaders. Competition between the three armed forces is an old Argentine tradition, as are suspicion and intrigue.

At the base where the reporter drops this item of information, they are all worried about the image of their branch. They order their own intelligence service to inquire into the whereabouts of the children. The children are located; though the boy will never reappear, the girl is saved. It's been proved that the branch in question had no involvement in the kidnapping.

I recall some of the infinite varied miracles that saved lives during World War II. The incredible contrivances of underground caves, closets concealed in back of other closets, wells at the bottom of other wells, forged documents, Gentiles honored today in Jerusalem for having saved Jews by passing them off as Christians and as their own children, Jews hidden in convents. But on reading the statistics of the Nazi occupation in Europe, the numbers overwhelm individual accounts; they far exceed them.

Yes, it's true that one of the woman's children was saved. But it was impossible on a daily basis to invent tactics that worked.

In Argentina, too, the statistics of the year 1976 far exceed the miracles.

January 26, 1980. *The Economist,* volume 274, number 7117, devotes a special section to Argentina—its political, social, and economic aspects. The journalist Robert Harvey writes:

The use of official terrorism to counter ordinary terrorism made Argentina a more dangerous place than Chile

after its coup because the rules of the game, for the government's critics, were so ill-defined. A journalist, for example, might be given a wink by a minister to go ahead and publish an article criticizing an aspect of government policy. But he would not know whether a security service belonging to the army, or to the air force, or to the navy, or to the local military governor, or to the provincial governor, or independent of any of these, would or would not take umbrage. And even a top minister might be unable to help him if he was whisked off by a group of unknown men one night.

6

They order me to turn my back to the door. They blindfold my eyes. I'm "boarded up," as they say in police jargon—a "board" placed over my eyes. They take me from the cell. I walk a long stretch, shoved from behind and guided by someone who, every once in a while, grabs me by the shoulders and sets me in the direction I'm to go in. There are many twists and turns. Long afterwards, while under house arrest, I was told by a policeman that the span I covered was probably quite short and that I was being made to circle round and round the same spot.

I hear the sound of voices and have the impression of being in a large room. I assume that I'm going to be made to undress for a torture session. But they sit me down, clothed, and tie my arms behind me. The application of electric shocks begins, penetrating my clothing to the skin. It's extremely painful, but not as bad as when I'm laid down, naked, and doused with water. The sensation of the shocks on my head makes me jump in my seat and moan.

No questions are asked. Merely a barrage of insults, which increase in intensity as the minutes pass. Suddenly, a hysterical voice begins shouting a single word: "Jew ... Jew ... Jew!" The others join in and form a chorus while clapping their hands, as we did as children when the Tom Mix film came on the screen at the movies. We'd clap our hands and shout: "Picture . . . picture . . . picture!"

Now they're really amused, and burst into laughter. Someone tries a variation while still clapping hands: "Clipped prick . . . clipped prick." Whereupon they begin alternating while clapping their hands: "Jew . . . Clipped prick . . . Jew . . . Clipped prick. . . ." It seems they're no longer angry, merely having a good time.

I keep bouncing in the chair and moaning as the electric shocks penetrate my clothes. During one of these tremors, I fall to the ground, dragging the chair. They get angry, like children whose game has been interrupted, and again start insulting me. The hysterical voice rises above the others: "Jew . . . Jew. . . ."

I ask my mother why they hate us so. I'm ten years old. We live in one of the poor sections of Buenos Aires, in one room, my parents, my brother, and I. There are two beds, a table, and a closet. It's a large building, and my mother is worried because we're the only Jews. She keeps arguing about it with my father, but renting a room in the Jewish section—"the city," as my father calls it—is much more expensive. My mother believes that it's dangerous not to have Jewish friends.

We're in the courtyard, where each dwelling is allotted a place for its stove. The stoves are a kind of outdoor charcoal grill with room for two pots. When it rains, cooking is done inside the room on a "primus," a primitive little stove. I've just returned from the coal yard and place some charcoal on sheets of paper. My mother ignites the paper, for a child ought not to play with fire; but I'm put in charge of getting the coal to catch, assisted by a notebook I use to ventilate it.

There's much excitement in the building, for this is the weekend when Carnival festivities begin. I ask my mother if I can go in costume. We have no money to buy a costume, and I know it, but she's a good dressmaker. All the clothes my brother and I wear—pants, shirts, underwear—are sewn by my mother. The only things purchased for us are socks; shoes are generally a gift from some wealthy cousins. My mother could make me a clown's outfit out of white fabric. I could use an old sheet, the kind she lays over the table when ironing. The sheet could also serve as a pirate's cape, in which case I'd paint my face with a burnt cork.

The year is 1933, five years after our arrival from Russia. My mother says we're newcomers in Argentina, "greenhorns," but I don't feel like a newcomer. She talks to me in Yiddish, and I teach her Spanish. She learns, but goes on talking to me in Yiddish and calls me "Yankele." She shames me everywhere. But the Spanish translation also makes people smile: "Jacobo" is very Jewish. A relative had advised her when we entered the country to register me under the name of Alejandro, but my father was opposed to it.

I'm not to have a costume for Carnival, nor will I be allowed to play and celebrate in the street, for Carnival, according to my mother, is an anti-Semitic holiday. People disguise themselves in order to show that the Jews have no country, that they've been dispersed throughout the nations and dress in the clothing of other nationalities. But, says my mother, if I want to dress up in a costume, a nice holiday to do so and have a good time like honorable folk is Purim.

"And what costume will I wear at Purim?"

"I'll make you a costume as Herzl, or Tolstoy, both great men. You'll wear a beautiful beard, and look at the world with seriousness. And you'll recite words from some of the books they've written."

"But everyone will laugh at me."

"Only the goyim will laugh. Jews don't laugh at intelligent, studious people."

"Mother, why do they hate us?"

"Because they don't understand."

. . .

Yes, my mother in good faith believed that if the anti-Semites understood us, they'd stop hating us. But understand what? Our traditions? Our religion, our culture, our personality? She never told me.

One might suppose that I'm still asking the same questions a Jewish child of ten might ask, and exist in the realm of replies set forth by a humble Jewish woman who read with difficulty and held a very vague notion of the world. But from all the replies given to the ancient question of why we are hated, is there any more intelligent than another? Is there any one that's valid? I've never found an answer that even remotely suggests the well of anguish experienced by a person who feels hatred. I've not found one reply among philosophers, men of religion, or politicians.

Everything that's been written can illuminate only certain circumstances. The role of the Jew in various periods of history, the relationship of the Jew to production, culture, politics. The position of the Jew in slave society, in the Middle Ages, at the outbreak of the Renaissance. Jewish mobility in urban society, Jewish vitality in great revolutions. Jews who played a key role in the transition from one historical epoch to another. The reactions of non-Jews toward their own problems as catalyzed by their relationship with Jews. It has all been studied, digested, restudied, repeated, translated, studied again, prophesied, explained, and reclassified; and yet each time I approach the memory of that voice shouting "Jew" at me in a clandestine prison in Argentina, I still can't understand why an Argentine soldier who was combating leftist terrorism—irrespective of his methods—could feel such hatred against a Jew.

My mother was not the only one to assume that a good explanation could clarify her in the eyes of interrogating goyim. She was not the only one to assume that we were hated because we were not understood. In 1935, the Nazi government studied laws aimed at modifying the Jews' legal situation in Germany. Jewish community leaders published prominent notices in Berlin newspapers enumerating the names of Jews who had been decorated for their conduct in the ranks of the German army during World War I. The notices stated that the Jews were good German citizens and had proved it. But later, in September 1935, the Nuremberg Laws were passed nullifying German citizenship for all Jews. Jewish leaders in Germany believed that the crux of the problem stemmed from the Nazis' inability to understand them, and that the latter simply had to be informed that the Jews were good citizens, even a trifle militaristic, moreover xenophobic when it came to the French, as well as anti-Communistic.

In 1936, the Olympics were held in Berlin. Some members of the U.S. team were Jewish. They qualified for the Olympic Games and hoped to beat the German athletes. This would prove to the Nazis that there's no such thing as Aryan superiority and that the Jews are not inferior to other human beings.

During the preparation of this book I accumulated endless data, anecdotes, interpretations, statistics. Yet what use is there in reproducing it all, superimposing one more typographical deluge upon another, even though it be differently organized and selected? To take certain books that were written on the basis of other books, and to write yet another book; then what? Would the goyim understand and cease to hate us? Would Jews understand why we are hated?

I prefer to attempt a different approach, devoted exclusively to describing the imminent danger at this moment, in this period, and under present circumstances. Ignoring the diverse shadings within the interminable shifting hatreds among the different classes of society in this period. Signaling only the chief dangers, the chief hatred that can actually lead to extermination.

When the extreme Right combats its natural enemies, its most hated object is the Jew. Its hatred is focused upon the Jew. This hatred inspires the extreme Right, exalts it, elevates it to romantic, metaphysical heights. Its natural enemy is the Left, but its target of hatred is the Jew. When it comes to the Jew, hatred can branch off into something greater than the Marxist peril.

Directed toward the Jew, hatred can attain novel dimensions, original forms, whimsical colorations. Hatred toward the Jew needs no system, discipline, or methodology. All you need do is allow yourself to be carried along, allow the hatred to drag you, overwhelm you, imprint itself upon you, arouse your imagination, your phobias, your areas of impotence and omnipotence, reticence and impunity. Regardless of the magnitude or diversity of its hatred, members of the extreme Right can employ it in their relationship to the Jew without having to alter their final goal of fighting for a totalitarian society whose aim is extermination of the Left and of democratic forms of life.

When the extreme Left combats its natural enemies, it can color the rigidity of its stagnant political philosophy with variations based on international conspiracy, foreign influences, demagogic and opportunistic alliances. The messianism inherent in its analysis of the role that it's been called upon to play in society finds a necessary pawn in the Jew for its Manichaean game. It's the old story of Good and Evil, Revolution and Counterrevolution, and nothing can match the speed whereby a Jew is identified with Evil. It's easier to get a young Uzbek, who dreams of being able to wear blue jeans some day and see a John Wayne movie, to hate a Jew than an American. Hatred of the Jew adds a spicy and delicious ingredient to the struggle for World Revolution. An aura of mysterious forces, which can stir the fear and hatred instilled in our psyche and biology. The Jew can satisfy this quota of irrational hatred required by every human being, but which a systematized ideology such as the extreme Left is unable to acknowledge in its relationship with society. Therefore, why not leave the window open, at least a crack, to allow that hatred to filter in? And against whom else if not the Jew? Is it hard perhaps to pinpoint the Jew as the enemy? The mere fact that the extreme rightists seek to utilize him as *their* enemy is clear indication that he is not—that the Jew,

even in this area, plays a role that is at once confusing, mysti-
fying, and concealed. This fact in itself is an incitement, is it
not, to identify him more clearly and precisely?

I was held in three clandestine sites in Argentina, and two
legal prisons. I was able to exchange ideas with political prisoners prior to, during, and after my arrest. A curious fact
emerged: in Argentina, the attitude of military examiners or
police toward left-wing terrorists was the way you might feel
toward an enemy. Sometimes, because of the individual nature of the people involved, or a passing frame of mind, it was
even a relationship of mutual adversaries. These political
prisoners were not spared when it came to torture or murder; but the psychological relationship was simple—confrontation with one's enemy or adversary, and the desire to destroy, to eliminate, that individual.

With Jews, however, there was a desire to eradicate. Interrogating enemies was a job; but interrogating Jews was a
pleasure or a curse. Torturing a Jewish prisoner always
yielded a moment of entertainment to the Argentine security forces, a certain pleasurable, leisurely moment. At some
point, a joke would invariably interrupt the task and give way
to pleasure. Amid moments of hatred, when the enemy must
be hated in order for him to be broken, hatred of the Jew was
visceral, explosive, a supernatural bolt, a gut excitement, the
sense of one's entire being abandoned to hatred. Such hatred
was a deeper expression than the mere aversion aroused by
an enemy, for it expressed, in addition, the need for a hated
object and the simultaneous fear of that object—the almost
magical inevitability of hatred. One could hate a political
prisoner for belonging to the opposite camp, but one could
also try to convince him, turn him around, make him understand his error, switch sides, get him to work for you. But how
can a Jew be changed? That is hatred: eternal, interminable,
perfect, inevitable. Always inevitable.

No, there can be no doubt my mother was the one who was
mistaken. It is not the anti-Semites who must be made to
understand. It is we Jews.

. . .

We're at the military prison in Magdalena, in the province of Buenos Aires. I'm to be examined by a War Council presided over by an army colonel, and made up of two officers from each of the three branches of service. Before appearing, I'm to be detained in a military prison.

Since we prisoners are held incommunicado, only one of us is permitted to enter the shower at a time. But sometimes the guard gets fed up with the excessive control: opening a cell, leading the prisoner to the shower, waiting till he's washed, leading him back again to his cell, shutting the cell, opening another cell. . . . When this occurs, the guard passes along the corridor, opens all the cells, and tells us to remain standing naked at our door ready to go for a shower one at a time.

At one such point, a guard passes in front of an elderly Jew and makes a joke about his circumcised penis—his clipped prick. The Jew smiles, too, and blushes. As if apologizing. Or at least that's how it strikes the guard, who dismisses it with a gesture. The old man looks at me, again blushes, and I have the sense that he's trying to explain things to me.

Two successive glances, almost simultaneous. The guard imagines he's being asked forgiveness. I imagine that I'm being implored to understand. The guard forgives him. I understand him.

I've also spoken with Jewish prisoners from Soviet jails, and read their memoirs and articles. They too have confirmed that Communist interrogators have a different relationship with the enemy than they do with the enemy-Jew. The enemy can be converted; he wasn't born an enemy. The Jew was born a Jew.

In Russian jails, similarly, the wardens—sometimes good-natured, mustachioed and bearded peasants—will crack a joke with a Jewish prisoner. And the prisoner, similarly, feels ashamed for that inexplicable nature of his, that inexplicable place he occupies in the world and in reality.

If one reads transcripts of the long interrogations that dissident Russian Jews have undergone, it's possible to discern the precise moment at which the interrogation crosses the borderline of hope. Hope is something that belongs to the interrogator rather than to the prisoner. The interrogator always seems to feel that he can succeed in modifying the will of the interrogated. But in the case of Jews being interrogated, there comes a moment when one can perceive that the interrogator has lost all hope. And that moment coincides with a shift from general political topics to the theme of the Jew, the Jewish personality, the role that Jewish "ideology" plays in the interrogated prisoner.

Certainly I can perceive that difference when reading documents about Russian prisoners, and I saw it clearly when a shift occurred in the frame of mind of my own interrogators. Once they reached the Jewish theme, it was impossible to harbor any hope of resolution, for their lifelong opinions of Jewish designs were beyond modification, rooted in their existence and not in their political convictions.

Is Argentina an anti-Semitic country? No; no country is. But there are anti-Semitic factions operating in Argentina, as indeed there are in all other countries. Are they violent? More violent than some, less violent than others. And the military? Each time a military government comes into power in Argentina, typical anti-Semitic acts disappear (the bombs placed in synagogues and Jewish institutions), for a military government at the outset imposes a certain order. But the Jew as citizen senses that his situation is altering: military governments do not name Jews to public posts; state radio and television prefer not to hire Jews; and so on, although there are always a certain number of Jews designated to serve as a defense against any possible accusation of anti-Semitism.

But this is past history. The military government that took power in Argentina in March 1976 arrived with an all-embracing arsenal of Nazi ideology as part of its structure. It would be impossible to determine whether this was backed by the majority or minority of the armed forces, though unquestionably anyone who was a Nazi, or merely anti-Semitic, didn't have to conceal or disguise his feelings; he could act accordingly. Security forces could repress Jews simply because they were Jews. They could mistreat political prisoners for their politics as well as for being Jews. The secret services could prosecute individuals, basing accusations simply on the fact that they were Jews; the leaders of the repression could detain Jewish prisoners merely for the pleasure of having Jewish prisoners, without any need to stipulate a valid accusation against them.

This outbreak of anti-Semitism prompts a fresh approach to Argentina, but one no different from that historically familiar from other countries, episodes, and examples. When confronted by an eruption of anti-Semitic violence, whether avowed or disguised, explicit or implicit, no one helps the Jews—and, generally, not even the Jews themselves help one another. At least, not those in the country where it transpires. Once more the fact is confirmed, as in other countries, that in the face of irrational violence, anti-Semites find both allies and the indifferent, but seldom any appreciable number of opponents.

Judging from my experiences in Argentina of recent years, I'd say that the armed forces and trade unions could potentially become involved in extremely intense anti-Semitic activity if socioeconomic conditions allow. Political parties and the press will in all likelihood demonstrate indifference. Argentine Jews may then try to adjust to conditions without a struggle, passively accepting their reduced rights and the increasingly severe restrictions on ghetto territory. The Catholic Church will most probably stand alone in denouncing racism publicly. And, of course, there will always be a few suicidal individuals to join the Church in this battle.

Many times I've been asked whether a Holocaust is conceivable in Argentina. Well, that depends on what is meant by a Holocaust, though no one would have been able to answer such a question affirmatively in 1937 in Germany. What you can say is that recent events in Argentina have demonstrated that if an anti-Semitic scenario unfolds, the discussion on what constitutes anti-Semitism and persecution and what does not will occupy more time than the battle itself against anti-Semitism. It's hard to foresee whether by then it will be too late or whether there will still be time to salvage something.

If we cared to formulate a historical equation, we could say that the conditions do exist: a profound political crisis, an economic crisis with an annual 170 percent rate of inflation that has lasted for several years, impotence on the part of political parties to come up with a minimally coherent response, the incapacity of the Jewish community to face straightforwardly its own reality, a totalitarian mentality among the majority sectors of the population, with a serious tendency toward messianic beliefs. If the outbreak of anti-Semitism has not until now assumed greater and more pronounced characteristics, this is because the balance of power within the armed forces has been under permanent debate in recent years, with the moderates weighing the potential international repercussions and concluding that these would be hard to withstand. But perhaps the Holocaust is in a way already occurring, as if the seeds were already planted. It depends on one's view of anti-Semitism—or of a Holocaust. There are no gas chambers in Argentina, and this leaves many with a clear conscience. Yet between 1974 and 1978, the violation of girls in clandestine prisons had a peculiar characteristic: Jewish girls were violated twice as often as non-Jewish girls. (Must all anti-Semitism wind up in soap? If so, then anti-Semitism does not exist in Argentina, and it becomes a matter of accidental, coincidental situations, as the leaders of the Argentine Jewish community claim. But can there be anti-Semitism without soap? In that case, the

Jewish community leaders are no different from the Judenrat of the Hitler ghettos at the beginning of the Holocaust.)

No one can predict what will happen in the future to the 400,000 Argentine Jews. But everyone knows that something terrible has already happened in recent years when you consider two facts: that the repression took place in the second half of the 1970s, not 1939; and that nothing equal to it had taken place in the Western world since 1945, with the end of World War II. Each side offers its own explanation:

The government explanation: The Jews are free to engage in any activity in Argentina. They can leave and enter the territory as often as they wish; there is no discrimination against them. Episodes of torture of arrested Jews or specific violation of Jewish girls are isolated, and not government policy; no prisoners are arrested by virtue of being Jewish.

The explanation of Jewish community leaders: All this is certainly true, but the isolated episodes exceed government claims. Some Jews have been arrested without any formal accusation, or even an informal accusation that would be inadmissible in court. It's best to work in silence in order to ransom whomever you can, rather than create scandals that might provoke the military.

A curious dichotomy exists. Argentine Jews are prepared to renounce many more rights and much more respect than the military believe; and the military for their part are much more fearful than the Jews realize of some kind of public Jewish self-defense. Provided that it *is* of a public nature.

I've often asked myself whether democrats believe in the existence of Naziism. The slogans, ideology, beliefs, and myths of Naziism sound so absurd that it's impossible to conceive of Nazis acting with perfect rationality, convinced of their logic, constructing an internal coherence that links events and ideology until it produces hallucinatory results.

The Argentine government steadfastly insisted that I was not arrested for being a Jew, nor for being a journalist. Never,

however, did it indicate why I was arrested or give any reasons for my arrest. At least, there was no official statement,
no accusation filed against me.

If, therefore, I were to venture an explanation besides the
fact that *La Opinión*'s existence had become intolerable to
the extreme sector, which is simply a political interpretation,
the only concrete element at my disposal, the only objective,
palpable element, would be the long, interminable interrogations they put me through. These interrogations are a clue
to what they were looking for, and therefore to the motive
for my arrest.

Any totalitarian interrogator—whether he be Nazi or
Communist—has a definite conception of the world he in-
habits and of reality. And any fact that fails to conform to this
conception is suitably distorted in order to fit into the
scheme. Distorted or explained, judged or restructured. For
that reason, perhaps, those who hold a fluid, pluralistic view
of reality may find certain convictions quite implausible that
to totalitarians seem natural and convincing. There's a ring
of absurdity to it when you read about it, but a much more
terrible aspect when you hear it in the context of an interrogation unraveling under the auspices of expert torturers.

It sounds absurd to read that my torturers wanted to know
the details of an interview they believed Menachem Begin
had held in 1976 in Buenos Aires with the Montoneros guerrillas. It's less absurd when you're being tortured to extract
an answer to that question. To anyone at all familiar with
Begin, such an interview sounds unreal. But it seems quite
coherent to someone who believes in the existence of an
international Jewish conspiracy prepared to utilize any
method to seize world power. The question then obeyed a
perfect logic:

1. In various raids of the security forces on residences that
had been occupied by Montoneros supporters, copies were
found of the Spanish edition of Begin's book, *Revolt in the
Holy Land*. Many of the paragraphs where Begin details
anti-British terrorist activities were underlined.

2. A guerrilla instruction manual found in Buenos Aires recommended Begin's book as source material on terrorist operations.

3. Begin was in Buenos Aires before he became Prime Minister.

4. An interview had taken place. Where?

How would one answer this question? For many years, Argentine Nazi ideologues have claimed the existence of a Jewish scheme for seizing Patagonia, the southern zone of the country, and creating the Republic of Andinia. Books and pamphlets have appeared on this subject, and it's extremely difficult to convince a Nazi that the plan is, if not absurd, at least unfeasible. Naturally, my questioners wanted to know more details than were presently available to them on this matter.

Question: We'd like to know some further details on the Andinia Plan. How many troops would the State of Israel be prepared to send?

Answer: Do you actually believe in this plan, that it even exists? How can you imagine 400,000 Argentine Jews being able to seize nearly 1 million square kilometers in the southern part of the country? What would they do with it? How would they populate it? How could they defeat 25 million Argentines, the armed forces?

Question: Listen, Timerman, that's exactly what I'm asking you. Answer me this. You're a Zionist, yet you didn't go to Israel. Why?

Answer: Because of a long chain of circumstances, all personal and familial. Situations that arose, one linked to the other, that caused me to postpone it time after time. . . .

Question: Come on, Timerman, you're an intelligent person. Find a better answer. Let *me* give an explanation so that we can get to the bottom of things. Israel has a very small territory and can't accommodate all the Jews in the world. Besides, the country is isolated in the midst of an Arab world. It needs money and political support from all over the world. That's why Israel has created three power centers abroad. . . .

Answer: Are you going to recite the Protocols of the Elders of Zion to me?

Question: Up to now, no one's proved that they're untrue. But let me go on. Israel, secure in these three centers of power, has nothing to fear. One is the United States, where Jewish power is evident. This means money and political control of capitalist countries. The second is the Kremlin, where Israel also has important influence. . . .

Answer: I believe the exact opposite, in fact.

Question: Don't interrupt me. The opposition is totally fake. The Kremlin is still dominated by the same sectors that staged the Bolshevik Revolution, in which Jews played the principal role. This means political control of Communist countries. And the third center of power is Argentina, especially the south which, if it were well developed by Jewish immigrants from various Latin American countries, could become an economic emporium, a food and oil basket, the road to Antarctica.

Each session lasted from twelve to fourteen hours; the interrogations began unexpectedly, and always dealt with subjects of this sort. The questions were impossible to answer. In my fatigue and exhaustion, I tried not to engage in ideological discussions so as to avoid the trauma of direct questions and impossible replies.

Why should the publisher of a newspaper who had devoted his entire career to political journalism in Argentina confess openly to being a Zionist? This was suspect. But then everything about me aroused suspicion.

Why, when rumors of my possible arrest began to circulate, hadn't I left the country? This too was suspect. Obviously, I'd been left behind for some mission.

Why as a political journalist had I hobnobbed so often with the military? A natural event in a country where politics basically stems from the barracks, but something that struck them as suspicious.

Which branch of the Jewish conspiracy did I belong to— the Israeli, Russian, or North American? A true dilemma, since I was born in Russia, had traveled to Israel, and was extremely friendly with the U.S. Embassy.

At any cost, they found it necessary for me to declare myself a Marxist. This demanded many hours of questioning and harsh treatment, without my being able to make them understand the obvious contradiction between being a Zionist and being a Marxist, according to their understanding of Marxism. Finally they accepted my declaration of being a Zionist, but one who employed Marxism as a dialectical tool to explain the contradictions of society.

I believe that in upper army echelons they finally acknowledged that Marxism and Zionism were mutually exclusive, yet still couldn't understand what Zionism was. Each time the subject was broached, they didn't quite know how to focus on it, and felt it might prove one of the pressing problems to be resolved after the battle against subversion was won.

Perhaps it was decided finally to shelve this compelling issue for more urgent problems having to do with the balance of power, the economic crisis, and inflation. Besides, they may have assumed that the incorporation of enforced Catholic education—for Jews as well—would suppress many exotic ideologies such as Zionism within the school curriculum.

Nevertheless, at the time of my arrest in 1977, the subject of Zionism obsessed them. Sometimes, outside the framework of formal questioning, they'd converse with me through the bars of my cell on Zionism and Israel, trying to accumulate information, taking notes. I advised them to go

to the Jewish Agency for more information than I was able
to provide from memory in my present physical state. This,
they said, might be too compromising. I thought they were
joking, but the subject, in their opinion, was inordinately
serious and genuinely obsessed them.

On one occasion, I was unexpectedly brought before the
Minister of the Interior. That day Patricia Derian, Assistant
Secretary of State in Washington for human rights and adviser to President Carter, had held an interview with President Videla during which she raised, with some vehemence,
the issue of my predicament.

The Minister of the Interior, who was concerned, wanted
to see with his own eyes what state I was in. We'd known
each other for years. Our conversation was long, but in no
way transcendent. Only one point was noteworthy. I told
him that I'd been informed I would be brought before a War
Council, but I had not been told on what grounds or charges.
I wanted to know whether this information was correct. He
said that it was, but not to worry, since I was not a subversive
and would not be convicted by the War Council. Why, then,
was I being imprisoned?

Minister: You admitted to being a Zionist, and this point
                was revealed at a meeting of all the generals.
Timerman: But being a Zionist is not forbidden.
Minister: No, it isn't forbidden, but on the other hand it
                isn't a clearcut issue. Besides, you admitted to it.
                And the generals are aware of this.

The fact that this prejudice existed among the upper echelons was of enormous concern to me, and I managed to alert
the president of the Jewish community. In fact, he was already aware of it, having been personally informed by the
minister, who had mentioned to him that the Zionists were
extracting "blood and money" from Argentina for Israel. Yet
I was never able to convince this leader to open the issue to
public debate, allowing the entire community to participate

publicly and inviting leaders who were prepared to debate openly with the military.

His reply to me was that it was best to handle it on a personal level: he was accepting the further reduction of ghetto borderlines.

While in clandestine prisons, I was almost always cloistered in a cell close to the torture chamber. This was especially painful, even when they'd ceased torturing me. Once I heard the screams of a woman being tortured because she was a Jew, though she kept insisting that she was Catholic and that her family name was German.

Long afterward, in recalling this episode, I realized that at least that woman had a last line of defense—she could claim that she wasn't Jewish. But what could a Jewish woman have done in her stead?

The Jewish question dominated all the interrogations during my entire imprisonment. And although the government, its officials, and military personnel time and again put forth the most dissimilar explanations regarding my arrest, while never formulating a concrete accusation, the enormous undercurrent of irrational hatred behind these explanations, having no correlation with the words employed, could not deceive a Jew. It smelled of profound anti-Semitism, and the magnitude of their hatred increased along with the impossibility they faced of expressing that hatred openly and explicitly.

I had ample time to speculate on the Jewish reality against its contemporary background. Not so much because of my preoccupation with anti-Semitism, but because it was evident that Argentine Jewry, like world Jewry, seemed incapable of responding to this level of aggression at its moment of occurrence and with a speed matching the speed at which Judaism was attacked. My younger son, in fact, was studying the topic of anti-Semitism at the Hebrew University in Jerusalem. While under house arrest, I wrote him that I didn't think any sociologist, politician, or philosopher could determine when anti-Semitism might disappear from the earth. I said that our task was not to convince the anti-Semites or to exterminate them, but to prevent anti-Semites from destroying us.

So, when I saw that Argentine Jewish leaders refused to focus on the issue in its true dimensions, and began to recognize the extent of Jewish passivity, I was stunned—amazed, almost unable to encompass it, trying to unearth some elusive clue. Then gradually I became poisoned by hatred and vindictive desires. I would forget my torturers, I declared, but never the Jewish leaders who acquiesced calmly in the torturing of Jews. During a visit from the Israeli leader Yigal Allon, while I was under house arrest in Buenos Aires, I told him that I had not been humiliated by torture, by electric shocks on my genitals, but had been profoundly humiliated by the silent complicity of Jewish leaders. My incarceration and torture were a personal tragedy, but nothing more, for in view of the sort of journalism I practiced, the possibility of my arrest and assassination fit into the rules of the game. Whereas the panic of Argentine Jewish leaders constituted a nightmare within the tragedy. And it was that nightmare that agonized me and kept me awake.

Of course, there's still the typical statement I heard so often: Even if I had not been a Jew, I would have been assassinated because of the nature of the work I was involved in. That may be. After all, Hitler also sent homosexuals, gypsies, Communists, and others to concentration camps. But the Jews were sent as Jews. Something similar occurred and is still occurring in the Russian Gulags—all one need do is read the interrogations of dissident Jews in the Soviet Union.

So, what can we do? One point has already been proved: Everything that happened once can happen again. And in the case of Argentina, the Jews' historical memory functioned belatedly, slowly, and then possibly only because a well-known Jew was involved. But what is to be done for those who are still imprisoned—without accusation, without trial—enduring amiable anti-Semitic jokes or anti-Semitic rages, dependent wholly on the guard who happens to be on duty that day?

It is best, I believe, not to elaborate extensively on this, but to return to simpler truths. I was never able to prove to my interrogators that Zbigniew Brzezinski was not a Jew or the head of the Latin American Jewish conspiracy, or that Sol Linowitz was not second in command and I his Argentine representative. Some things cannot be proven. And one of them, it strikes me, is the right of Jews to exist. Simply speaking, the only thing one can do is fight for one's own right to exist. Under certain circumstances, anti-Semitic groups seize power in a country—or exercise a portion of that power. It may be for a long or a brief while. Argentina is in the former stage, and all the conditions exist for this to be a rather prolonged stage. That is certain. The other fact that's certain is that the Argentine Jewish community is not about to defend itself. And, finally, one further indubitable fact: The international community is able to intervene, via innumerable mechanisms, in order to disseminate this information, particularly in Argentina. Only public knowledge can alter, to some extent, the course of these events, this downward slope in the march of history.

In order to strengthen the Jewish spirit, people often resort to observations on the tragic fate that has accompanied their existence. I've learned, however, that the only thing that strengthens the Jewish spirit is understanding plus a sense of identity. Being is more important than remembering. I believe that the reminder of Jewish tragedies, punctiliously invoked by the Jewish community against its adversaries, has been futile in overcoming the paralysis and panic that envelop it. Those who succeeded in doing so in recent difficult years were impelled, and are impelled, by a clear notion of their Jewish identity. Only Zionism is capable of providing this identity with a movement, dynamic, and policy. On different occasions, since my release and even at times during interrogation, I was asked how I would have been treated had the Trotskyite or Perónist terrorists seized power there. I have no doubts. I would have been placed against a wall and shot, following a summary trial. The charge: counterrevolutionary Zionism.

In this respect, as in so many others, Fascists of the Left and Right complement each other. They need, and agree with, one another.

7

The peephole of my cell opens and the face of the corporal on guard appears. He smiles, and tosses something into the cell. "Congratulations, Jacobo."

This is the first time anyone has spoken to me. Until now, the discipline in this place to which I was brought a few days ago has been extremely severe. With each change of guard, the light is turned on from outside and they shout out: "Name?" This means that the peephole gets opened four times a day, every six hours. I'm cursorily addressed at other times, when the three dishes of hot liquid that constitute breakfast, lunch, and dinner are delivered. The peephole is opened, and I'm asked: "Are you going to eat?"

So the guard's present remark is startling. My initial reaction, whenever a new event occurs, is always: What will happen to me now? True, I'm in a legal prison at central headquarters of the Federal Police in Buenos Aires. The cell measures nearly two meters in width and three in length. Furthermore, it has a privy in it so that I needn't ask permission to go to the toilet, and it has a tap with drinking water. I can also wash up, but have no soap or towel. There's a cement bed without mattress, though I was promised one. I have a blanket, but gusts of cold air penetrate from the space

above the wall, and I must walk for hours in an attempt to
keep warm. If I calculate carefully the longest diagonal ex-
tending from the hole in the ground to the other end of the
cell, I'm able to take seven steps. I've already covered a
thousand laps.

It's better, much better, than in a clandestine prison. But
no one talks to me. I don't know what's going to happen; the
peephole is always shut. Everything is utterly still, except for
the sounds and voices that penetrate from outside. Before
dawn, while it's still dark, I can hear the bugle, commanding
orders, and the sound of a formation under my window.
Then the sounds of courtyards being washed; also tin pots.
This takes place alongside what might be called the window
—a mere hole in a wide wall, with a double row of iron bars.
I climb on the bed to look outside, but am unable to see
anything because the wall is so thick. From the corridor on
the other side of the peephole, I can also hear shouts—not
commands but insults. Prisoners, no doubt, washing the passageway and being yelled at and struck by the corporal.
Often I hear prisoners weeping. One of the punishments
meted out to those who don't do a good scrubbing job is to
force them to undress, lean over with their index finger on
the ground, and have them rotate round and round, dragging their finger on the ground without lifting it. This is
called "looking for oil." You feel as if your kidneys are burst-
ing. But it's even more entertaining to place a prisoner near
the wall and have five hefty policemen form a little train by
lining up in single file and holding onto the hips of the person
in front. They come down the passage making the sound of
a locomotive and, picking up speed, hurl themselves like a
dead weight on the prisoner, plastering him against the wall.
This is called the "choo-choo shock." When they're busy,
though, they simply order the prisoner to run naked along
the passageway, which is fifty meters from one end to the
other, reciting aloud sayings dictated to him. He has to repeat these without stopping until they invent others. *My
mother's a whore. . . . The whore who gave birth to me.*

. . . I masturbate. . . . I must respect the corporal on guard. . . . The police love me. . . .

The prisoner who is incommunicado is envious of all this. He longs to see a face. His need engenders a series of skills. From his isolation, he begins to comprehend the architecture of the outside world, a faceless architecture that he pieces together like a puzzle. Although he is a blind man, a dextrous blind man who comes to the end of his task without a happy conclusion providing him any relief, he remains, in the end, blind, never able to see the vital part. There are long silences that must be linked with whispers. (A soft voice asks, "Who's there?" and, softly, I reply, "Timerman," and the voice lets out a burst of laughter. Then another voice slowly asks, "Who's there?" and this time I don't answer; but another time I say, "Timerman," and he murmurs, "Be strong.") Then, too, one must find a place in the puzzle for the shouts, insults, and hard beatings meted out to prisoners, the jokes toward homosexuals; all must be incorporated in order to have an idea of what's going on. The police need to shout— shouting helps them. They have orders from their superiors to shout all the time in order to intimidate and confuse prisoners. Therefore, whenever they talk, they shout, which adds to the puzzle, to the effort of constructing the outside world, the only world apart from the cell.

And then there are other pieces: The policeman who negotiates with a homosexual to rent a cell in the isolation ward so that the latter can receive alternating prisoners from another ward, the one for petty criminals and thieves who are in for sixty or ninety days, entitled to use their money for food, and glad to pay for this hour of male prostitution inside a cell located in the heart of Buenos Aires, a hallucinatory brothel administered by the Federal Police, which Juan Domingo Perón pronounced the best police force in the world.

Adding further to the puzzle are the big cleaning days when a commissioner will be coming for inspection and the cells are disinfected. But since those who are held incommunicado cannot be let out, a man in white opens the door and fumigates the cell with puffs of white powder. The chemical smell engulfs me for days, though I no longer fear choking, like the first time. Then there are the typical Sunday sounds, when the names of prisoners with visiting rights are called out, and you hear radio broadcasts of soccer matches and smell the odor of different foods, that of the guards no doubt; there are days, too, when you hear the droning sound of a religious service.

And that is why I am startled now. The sound that just dropped into my cell has destroyed the puzzle and doesn't fit into the despair of the cell, nor into my effort to compensate for that despair by my slow, laborious, ardent reconstruction of the exterior architecture, the blind man's stubborn obsession with his puzzle.

I pick up a letter and two candies. The letter, a few brief lines, is from my wife. Dated May 20, 1977. We've been married today for twenty-seven years. I leave everything on the bed and go back to my task as blind architect: She's undoubtedly contacted one of our army friends, one of those who came to our house so often, or one of the retired officers who worked on my newspaper, perhaps someone who spent vacations at our beach house. . . . And yet, this doesn't fit into the heightened sensibility of a blind man whose sightless eyes are gazing at an unknown world. No military man nowadays would dare to speak to my wife. More likely one of the policemen, a ward guard, went to visit her and offered, for a sum of money, to bring something to me. At this point the blind architect starts reconstructing the scene. My house, the entrance, the doorbell, my wife's face. . . . But no, the image of my wife's face is unbearable in this place.

How I cursed my wife that day! How many times I told myself I wouldn't read her letter, I wouldn't eat the candies. After so many efforts to forget, to refrain from loving and desiring, to refrain from thinking, the entire painstaking edifice constructed by the blind architect collapses over his head. Already I'd begun to belong to the world around me, the one I actually belonged to, the imprisoned world where my heart and blood were installed: this world I've already accepted and that is real, that corresponds to the inscriptions on the wall, the odor of the latrine matching that emitted by my skin and clothes, and those drab colors, the sounds of metal and violence, the harsh, shrill, hysterical voices. And now this world, so heavily armored, so solid and irreplaceable, without cracks, has been penetrated by a letter and two candies. Risha, why have you done this to me?

She tells me that if she could she'd give me heaven with all its stars and clouds, all the air in the world, all her love, all her tenderness. She says that she'd kiss me a thousand times if she could. But that is what she fails to understand: she cannot. In a rage, I throw the letter into the latrine, and with equal rage stick the two candies into my mouth. But already I'm lost, for the flavor is overpowering, as is my wife's face, her scent almost; and my realization that I've been married today for twenty-seven years and have been sequestered for forty days.

How can a blind architect fit into his unknown edifice— that structure he can neither see nor touch—the face of his wife, the taste of two candies, his wedding anniversary? Anywhere I place them, the structure collapses. Then, once again, I sit down on the stone bed, and when the guard opens the peephole to ask me my name, once again I arouse myself from the submerging debris, grasping for a life jacket to reconstruct my reality. I don't reply, and the guard kicks the steel door with his heavy boots. "Name, son of a whore!"

The blind architect goes to work trying to fit the meaning of this insult into his world. He no longer needs to remember. At this juncture I feel as if I've passed the first serious test, worse than torture, and that I'll survive. For it is here that you must survive, not in the outside world. And the chief enemy is not the electric shocks, but penetration from the outside world, with all its memories.

. . .

I get into a big black car, the back seat. It's raining in New York. I've been free barely a month. Liv Ullmann also gets in. I'm occupying the wide back seat, and she seats herself in one of the small fold-up seats that provide extra places. We've just attended a lecture by Elie Wiesel, and are on our way to a gathering of friends at someone's home.

She gazes at me with sympathy, indifference, or perhaps aloof interest. And I look at her with hatred. But my voice is calm, dispassionate in tone, maybe even indifferent. Yet it would be impossible not to tell her that it was she, Liv Ullmann, who did me the most harm while I was in prison. I tell her almost everything, perhaps a bit less, or perhaps now I am telling her less than before or find more to say than before. We called her "Howlmann" because her name coincided with the word "howl," which was what we mostly did in our cells—we howled inside, inverting biology and sounds. And all this happened after her book arrived in the prison.

She destroyed the blind architect, revealing his full misery, terror, and horror to him; she brought the crows that would devour every part of his accumulated vital blood; she incited him to hatred, death, madness. She didn't spare him one iota of despair. She revealed the bruises on his legs; she dispelled the haze he'd been slumbering in; she awakened every fragment of his paralyzed brain, of his dormant memory; she unfolded before his single seeing eye the colors of the fever of love, of lips to be kissed, of slender fingers, little fingers, the soft, tiny fingers of her daughter Linne.

She brought to that place where tenderness is the enemy, where goodness is madness and memory the implacable, encroaching leper, she brought that gentle face of hers, enhanced by photography and Renaissance type, with those real eyes and lips, and that word "Changing," an absurd word for a prisoner, plus that relationship with her daughter. She brought it directly to me—me with three sons, and I tremulously defended myself against their memory, those three sons who'd been told by a policeman that their father was a brave man because of the manner in which he withstood torture.

I tell her these things in that automobile crossing Manhattan in the rain, in the autumn of 1979, or perhaps other things, or not even those, refraining possibly from mentioning the men who remained behind, who likewise hate her. Liv Ullmann starts to tremble, and a woman psychiatrist at my side begins to cry, then tells me if I need help to call her. And many times in the hotel, with her white card on my table, I've thought of telling Erika Padan Freeman how much I hated that Norwegian of Swedish fame, that woman so proud of her tenderness—much more than I conveyed to her as we were squeezed into an American millionaire's car.

In fact, I don't think I even tell Liv Ullmann that I hate her, only that her book did me harm. It was brought by someone to my cell after I was no longer incommunicado, and was allowed to see my family every day for five minutes. We were permitted to receive books and newspapers but no food, though my children used their ingenuity in hiding small bits of chocolate, cake, or candy inside their trousers, socks, jackets, and sleeves. On that particular day, the only thing I tell Liv Ullmann about that desolate place where everything is somehow surmountable through psychological subterfuge, where one's relationship with his torturer at times even has the aspect of an encounter between two human beings, where marriages exist between men in which pity infuses their encounter . . . the only thing I tell her is that tenderness there is nonexistent. There is a total absence of tenderness, and it's impossible to create it via any subterfuge. No one gives tenderness, and no one receives it. It's impossible to go beyond pity, and it is with pity that a prisoner adds to his armature of feelings and sensations.

When two prisoners shake hands it's an act of pity, as is the apple once given me and which I subsequently threw, while walking in the corridor during recreation break, into someone's isolation cell whose peephole was open. A cake of borrowed soap, a gift of underpants—that is pity. Listening for hours to the babble of someone who has been tortured to force him to reveal the hiding place of his son, who he later discovers has "disappeared"—that is pity. To show interest in the plans of an architect who may soon be released and who still retains intact his ideals on urbanization, housing developments, creativity in support of neighborhood groups—that is pity.

But that is all. There is no tenderness. The five-minute family visit is filled with caresses, whispered words, kisses given in full view of everyone. Yet there is no surrender to tenderness, no brimming, unstinting tenderness, no unbridled, fearless tenderness; only a suggestion of it conveyed in moderation to remind you that it's there. But the biology of survival is also there, and the intoxication of tenderness is tantamount to death, madness, suicide.

Liv Ullmann's book appeared in this place like a mockery, with its impudence, the omnipotence of someone able to give and receive tenderness; with its insolence, of someone able to enjoy and suffer tenderness; with its pleasure and pain devoid of pathos. Unencumbered by the risk of life, as ours were risked whenever tenderness appeared.

What need did she have to address us prisoners with that lighthearted cunning, that girlish mischievousness by which she describes herself and her relationship with her daughter? Lingering tenderly on landscapes, bodies, souls, meals—wielding tenderness like a screwdriver to open and penetrate, hurling it in our faces, while we prisoners were merely trying, with the aid of pity, to structure our own survival.

The thought of suicide occurred to me often. But I discovered then that it was a temptation rather than a premeditated decision. The idea of suicide, its temptation, would appear like a delicious fruit in situations where only death could arouse some sensation of desire. But the opportunity for suicide did not arise during those early weeks of interrogation and torture.

With hands bound behind me and eyes blindfolded, suicide was the only thing that could share the long endless

stretch of time, made up of time and more time, of interrogation and time, of cold and time, of hunger and time, of tears
and time. How to fill those orifices of time if not with the
preserved fruit of suicide? How to modify the rigid endless
structure of time if not with the unforeseen originality of
suicide?

With hands bound behind me and eyes blindfolded, there
was no possibility of suicide. I was transferred from my clandestine prison to the interrogators at police headquarters in
the city of La Plata, blindfolded, bound, thrown to the floor
in back of a car, covered with a blanket.

It was early in the morning by the time one of the longer
sessions, lasting I think about eighteen hours, was over. Accompanied by two guards, I was leaving La Plata and heading back in the direction of the clandestine prison. They
were exhausted but happy: I'd signed a declaration admit-
ting that I was a leftist Zionist. They sat me in back, alone,
did not blindfold me or tie me up, and gave me an apple.
They said that before reaching the prison, they'd cover me
with a blanket so that I wouldn't see the location, which was
known in their coded language as the Puesto Vasco. They
speeded along the deserted route while I, in absorption,
gazed through the window at the road. One of the guards
wanted to know what crazy thoughts were passing through
my mind as we heard a radio newscast announcing that
my wife had presented a new writ of habeas corpus to ascer-
tain my whereabouts. Smiling, I told him I was thinking of
opening the door and throwing myself from the car. But
he warned me not to attempt this because there obviously wouldn't be enough time—he'd grab me with his
hands, and I wouldn't have the strength to move. Again he
smiled, and said: "There were seventeen in this car, Jacobo."
It's for those seventeen faces that I had also to seek haven
in the night.

Aside from suicide, there's one other temptation—madness. These are the only two temptations, or rather the only
two strong emotions I experienced during my thirty months

of imprisonment and beatings. Strong emotions because their repressed violence enables them to overpower time. And time is not an easy enemy.

To reflect on suicide does not mean that you're going to commit suicide, or decide that suicide ought to be committed. It means introducing into your daily life something that is on a par with the violence around you. Managing to introduce into that daily life an element on the same level as the violence of that other element. It's like living on an equal footing with one's jailers, those who beat and martyr you. Sharing with oneself a non-inferior capacity, one equal in magnitude to that of one's oppressor. This self-imposed state of equality functions as a compensatory mechanism. It's with you, has the force to be with you, is created and structured in that place, that prison, and will afterwards be missed or remembered.

More than a decision or a hope, it's an occupation—its dimension so profound, so biological and awesome, that it's a palpable presence. Impossible to confuse with any other sensation, it introduces the possibility of achieving a level of destruction akin to the destruction unremittingly being inflicted upon you.

The word "suicide" is not linked, in the mind of the beaten and tortured prisoner, with any other connotation. Nor to the consequences, possibilities, remorse, or pain that it will produce, or the defeats that the act presumes. It is simply what it is, with its own taste, smell, form, and weight. And it fills the Time of the prisoner's time, and the Space of the prisoner's cell.

He can measure the wall-to-wall distance inside his cell and wonder whether his head will break if he hurls himself against that wall with all his might; or he can imagine the feasibility of puncturing a vein with his nails. All this inherent violence transmits a sensation of physical capacity and inevitability to the prisoner who's undergone torture. It contains an element of romantic audacity, the sense of a completed story.

There's pride in the idea of potential suicide. It's the primary temptation in response to the continual humiliation from one's torturers.

But at some point you must reach a decision to abandon the idea, for it can become too obvious a subterfuge. In fact, it already has become a subterfuge, for you realize that you're not going to commit suicide and once again comes the feeling of defeat. You're humiliated, and the humiliation is justified. Your world is utterly reduced, and the fact that you've told the torturers nothing, and that you've survived, doesn't occur to you. These are not usable values in this world of cockroaches, vomit dried on your clothes, bits of half-raw meat strewn on the ground. A world in which the sphincters must endure their gross intestinal content until you're authorized by a guard to go to the toilet.

Suicide is a usable value because of its definitive, hopeless nature. And can anyone within that obscurity of torture and darkness conceive that the place where he is, the space where he is, is anything other than definitive and irremediable?

Hence, when the possibility of suicide no longer exists, with its splendid image of a raging bull ready to confront the bullfighter's truth—that suicide which in the darkness of one's cell has the somber, austere, incorruptible flavor of vengeance—when that possibility of suicide no longer exists, there remains the temptation of madness.

Yes, the temptation of madness remains, though it's impossible to deal with madness as one does with suicide. You must await madness, and think that perhaps it will come. You must try to yield to it, and possibly it will engulf you. Await it and yield to it—that is the grim part. For if it fails to arrive, your impotence is conclusive, your humiliation greater than a kick on the behind from some voiceless, faceless stranger who leads you blindfolded, from your cell, stands you flat against the wall, gives you a kick in the ass, always in silence, then has you return to your cell with one of those delicate gestures suggested by the bejeweled hands of an El Greco painting.

Yes, punishment in silence leads to the temptation of madness. Yet madness is unavailable, and you can await it in vain. I waited for it one whole night—I believe that it was night —after a long torture session. I'd been transferred from Puesto Vasco to another location, and then taken to police headquarters in La Plata, and back again to Puesto Vasco, so that I would be confused and unaware that I was at Puesto Vasco and in the kitchen, where the torture was inflicted.

I awoke in that strange place and, in vain, awaited madness. I was seated with my eyes blindfolded and hands tied behind me. Close by—it seemed quite close—a barking dog had been tied up, and every once in a while at uncertain intervals I could hear soft steps, and then, near my ears, the crash of an iron tool striking a metal surface. My body trembled in agitation; sharp points, dazzling in their dizziness, settled in my brain.

The dog barked, more ferocious than ever. Protesting the metallic explosion, and correctly so, for he too had his rights.

Madness did not come. Later, when no longer incommunicado, I met some prisoners at Puesto Vasco. I told them I thought I was insane, and they convinced me it wasn't so. They assured me that I was simply somewhat confused, but that everything would fall back in place. One of them said: "Don Jacobo, keep going. That's the important thing, not to let them knock you down. If you keep going, everything will someday be resolved."

Yes, tenderness was the enemy.

I awaited the protective mantle of madness, but it did not come.

I was unable to tame the beautiful bull of suicide, nor did I fling myself on its horns or drench its back with my blood.

I kept going, and here I am.

8

A woman doctor is dragged by her hair, hands tied behind her, through the long corridor of a city hospital in Buenos Aires. The man dragging her is fat and dressed in civilian clothes. At a particular moment her legs are also bound, she's covered with a blanket, placed on a stretcher, and put into a small truck. About fifteen armed men participate in this procedure.

They arrived in three automobiles, entered without any identification documents, asked for the place where the doctor practiced her specialty, psychiatry, and then took her away. No one questioned that group of men as to who they were or whom they represented. No one intervened on behalf of the doctor. The hospital authorities, other professionals, nurses, patients, everyone knew what was going on.

During the first months after the armed forces' seizure of power in Argentina, no sector of the population suffered more from the wave of kidnappings and disappearances than psychiatrists. The intelligence services of the armed forces had reached the conclusion that psychiatrists knew many behind-the-scenes details about subversive urban guerrilla activities, and that the mission of certain psychiatrists was to bolster the spirits of guerrillas when they were depressed as a result of the hardships of clandestine life.

By what process does an intelligence officer in the Argentine armed forces arrive at the conviction that a psychiatrist with a patient linked in some way to subversive activity is privy to the guerrilla activities of that individual and his entire group?

The world of the Argentine armed forces is a closed, hermetic structure. Most of the officers' wives are the sisters or daughters of men in the military. Nearly all are related, and whenever there's a military regime, the civilians who participate are mostly relatives of the military or individuals who have frequented military circles, in precise anticipation of that moment when the armed forces will take power. In Argentina, a show of deference to the military has for fifty years been almost a political career in itself, yielding juicy benefits whenever a military coup takes place.

This pattern has separated the military from the most elemental currents of modern life, and has instilled in them a series of fantasies about the true meaning of the scientific, moral, literary, and religious elements that mankind has incorporated into its normal daily existence in recent decades. The ideology motivating the Argentine military stems more from a notion of the world they reject than from a world they would like to attain. They would be unable to pinpoint or outline the reality they care to see materialize in Argentina, but could quickly describe what it is that they hate. If asked what they want, their answer will be: a decent country, respectful of family life and patriotism. But ask them what they don't want, and then you'll be able to understand their view of the world and the difficulties they encounter when they must govern in accordance with such hatreds. On the other hand, as in every totalitarian mind, hatreds are transformed into fantasies and conform to a view of the world that matches these fantasies, and these very fantasies lead to the development of their operational tactics.

Thus there's nothing surprising, for example, about their assumption that the anti-militarist movies about Vietnam

produced by Hollywood are part of a global scheme to defend human rights. And when they discover that a producer,
actor, or director in one of these films is Jewish, or of the Left,
their thesis of world conspiracy involving Jews and the Left
is confirmed.

The chief obsession of the totalitarian mind lies in its need
for the world to be clearcut and orderly. Any subtlety, contradiction, or complexity upsets and confuses this notion and
becomes intolerable. Whereupon an attempt is made to
overcome the intolerable by way of the only method at hand
—violence. Recourse to politics, strategy, and the gradual
resolution of conflicts becomes unlikely. The power monopoly is at its disposal, and it employs this monopoly with utter
ruthlessness in its compelling need to simplify reality.

The president of the Argentine Federation of Psychologists was dragged by her hair through the hospital corridors
where she practiced her profession because—according to
the mentality of the Argentine military—an arrest with in-
tent to question, without infliction of violence, would have
been an acknowledgment of the validity and logic of her
existence. And this in turn would mean acknowledging the
existence of a world other than its own hermetic one. Which
is intolerable.

The Argentine military government officially imposed
strict moral codes of censorship on films, theatrical and literary works. It modified university curriculums, eliminating
majors in sociology, philosophy, and psychology. It forbade
the use of Freudian techniques in psychiatric services inside
state hospitals. It imposed obligatory Catholic education on
pupils in the secondary schools. In its formal aspects, this
would all suggest a reactionary or conservative conception of
reality.

But at the same time it strove to eliminate physically all
those who in any way participated in the world it wanted to
modify. A mere modification of sociology education was considered inadequate; it was preferable to exterminate those in
Argentina who at some future point might reimplant mod-

ern sociology. Based on this concept of physical extermination as a final solution to the problem of one's conception of the world, the government of the armed forces eliminated thousands of individuals in Argentina who had no relation with subversion, but who (according to the military) formed part of, or represented, that world which they found intolerable and incomprehensible, and who hence constituted the enemy.

In converting hatred into fantasy, the totalitarian mind is carried away by political hallucinations, whose extent may seem absurd to a logical, rational modern mind. Yet these political hallucinations determine courses of action that can lead to situations of unexplored violence, seemingly impossible in the contemporary world.

This kind of mechanism, during the late seventies, triggered off in Argentina an outbreak of violence that seemed inconceivable after the Nazi madness and the political hallucinations in Russia. It seemed inconceivable because its justification was based on the same arguments as those of Hitler and Stalin. It characterized the same enemies; felt persecuted by the same opponents; and elaborated the same fantasies.

In 1979, a novel by Valentin Pikul was published about the last years of czarist rule in Russia prior to World War I. The work incorporates new discoveries about court life and the role played by Rasputin, and contains details and anecdotes hitherto unknown. But the most interesting aspect is its thesis, and the fact that the author considers himself a historian rather than a novelist. The thesis goes as follows: Rasputin, the czar and czarina, as well as the court, were all pawns in a Zionist-Jewish conspiracy that aspired to destroy Russia.

In the need to provide its hatred with a historical, moral, or ideological formulation, the totalitarian mind transforms that hatred into a fantasy capable of reaching any conclusion regarding the enemy's characteristics. If in Communist Russia the Jew is an enemy because he's considered to be cosmopolitan, or an Israeli sympathizer, or unadjusted to a

Socialist society, then he can likewise serve—indeed, he must serve—as a receptacle for every sort of hatred. He must encompass one's total capacity for hatred. According to the totalitarian mind, the Jew in present-day Russia must be considered an enemy not only of socialism but of everything that is Russian, everything that has ever constituted Russia, to the point even of being accused as the enemy of the last Russian czars, despite the fact that the elimination of the czarist regime was simultaneously and enthusiastically lauded.

This mechanism of political hallucination—hatred transformed into fantasy—is what enabled Naziism, with all due "logic," to regard abstract art as the enemy of Aryan Germany because it destroyed the notion of the archetypal Nazi; or to consider a man of the Left to be linked to the Jewish capitalist conspiracy because of the "anti-German" label that the Jew imparted to leftist activity.

These political hallucinations also governed the Argentine armed forces, constituted their ideology, and simultaneously prevented them from consolidating an idea of their self-ordained mission. The unacceptable world determined their tactics. Although such mechanisms were easy to perceive in Naziism and less apparent but equally discernible in communism, in the case of Argentina two elements impeded their visibility. First of all, Argentina did not implement its thesis on an international scale; it remained a domestic affair in a country whose destiny was not of world interest. Second, Argentina is a land of euphemisms, and the government has decided never to acknowledge its use of violence or the reasons for using it.

Many journalists in Argentina tried to investigate the causes that led to the repression of modern psychiatry and the physical elimination of psychiatrists. All inquiries, however, could reach only approximate conclusions.

The fact is that members of the military do not resort to modern psychiatry when there's a family problem that warrants treatment from this branch of medicine. Generally, they will seek the aid of a Catholic priest, his counsel to patient and family, his invocation of patience. This is indicative of their distrust of psychiatrists, comparable to the distrust felt by the totalitarian mind toward the unknown and toward anything pertaining to the realm of ideas that doesn't revolve around Catholicism.

What may have actually happened, if the process can be reconstructed, is that the intelligence services during interrogations discovered that certain terrorists or guerrillas were either in individual or group treatment, generally of a Freudian orientation. Probing further in these interrogations, they compiled and analyzed the various replies, and came to the conclusion that militants resorted to psychology in search of solutions to concrete problems, or in order to resolve emotional instabilities. In their daily quest for fresh elements in the worldwide anti-Argentine conspiracy, and in their need to have that conspiracy provide ample formulation of their irrational hatred, it was merely a matter of time before psychiatry was incorporated into the conspiracy. The role of psychiatry, they concluded, was programmed by the Health Command of the guerrilla forces and functioned along the same principles as a doctor's extraction of a bullet or treatment of a wound. All the "stress" and fears of clandestine life that affect a terrorist are emotionally channeled by psychiatrists. Psychiatry conditions the urban terrorist to wage his clandestine battle.

The search for psychiatrists was immediately launched. And, as happened on other levels when an individual was found who conformed to their fantasies, that is, to their descriptions, they felt that their thesis was justified, which led to the death of scores of psychiatrists who had never seen a guerrilla in their lives.

The centralization of action based on particular phobias and buttressed by impunity, whereby corpses simply disappeared after interrogations, wreaked havoc particularly among psychiatrists, sociologists, journalists, and university students.

These phobias conformed to the ideology of the armed

forces and in turn imbued their operating tactics with such violence that all sectors of the population, with very few exceptions, preferred to ignore what was happening, even when it was totally pervasive and widely known—at least among political and religious leaders, newspaper publishers, and political journalists. It paved the way for the "postwar" era that will assuredly occur in Argentina, a situation identical to that of postwar Germany where it was hard to find a single German who would admit to having known about the existence of concentration camps, gas chambers, or crematorium ovens.

The incapacity of the Argentine military to formulate a structured ideology leads to their general acceptance of the phobias of reactionary groups, with whom they feel more closely aligned than the democratic sectors. This phenomenon has been often repeated in Argentine life. The recurrence of the pattern, plus the degree of violence that Argentina underwent in the decade prior to the armed forces takeover of 1976, led the military to accept as well the final consequences of Fascist ideology: physical extermination of whoever is considered the enemy. In other words, the Final Solution.

The official argument of the armed forces when they took over the government in March 1976 was not complex; subversion and public corruption were the enemies. Enemies, therefore, were easy to identify. And no one doubted that the methods would be those fixed by the Constitution, whose legal repressive scope was quite adequate. Yet the military in charge of repression seemed to require not merely an adequate margin for solving the problem, but also sufficient leeway to implement with impunity their phobias, fantasies, notions about reality, and vision of the future. Only communism or fascism could provide a solid program for embarking in the late seventies upon such an absolute violation of human values. Logically, they chose fascism. Other alternatives existed in the contemporary world, but they failed to conform to Argentine cultural, political, economic, and social standards. Violence based on a religious leadership, as with the Ayatollah Khomeini in Iran, or situations combining superstition, cannibalism, tribal struggle, as in Uganda or the Central African Empire, are inapplicable in a country like Argentina.

As publisher of *La Opinión*, I often attempted to correct the irrationality that had been converted into ideology by the armed forces in charge of repression. I had only one permanent, unswerving companion in this arduous battle: the English-language newspaper, the Buenos Aires *Herald*. Occasionally, some provincial papers joined our attempt to channel the Argentine military process within constitutional or juridicial norms; or certain Catholic publications, such as the magazine *Criterio*. This activity in some instances succeeded in saving a life, although it never actually modified the course of events. Almost a year before my detention, I learned that the military had resigned themselves, in the course of lengthy debates, to the existence of the English newspaper, but had decided to initiate steps leading to the suppression of *La Opinión*. In April 1977 I was detained, *La Opinión* confiscated, and the publisher of the Buenos Aires *Herald* forced, through a campaign of threats, to abandon Argentina in December 1979, although his newspaper was not successfully silenced.

In the interests of greater effectiveness, we often endeavored at *La Opinión* to attempt an objective approach to the ideology of the armed forces, though it was always impossible. It was clear that they hated Karl Marx, Che Guevara, Sigmund Freud, Theodor Herzl. But it was hard to understand that they hated Zionism more than communism, and considered it a more significant enemy; and that they regarded Israel as a more dangerous foe than Russia.

If someone were to discuss the subject privately with a military officer, he would obtain an explanation of sorts. Communism was more visible than Zionism, therefore easier to identify, and hence less dangerous, although both ideologies had as their ultimate intention the destruction of nationality. Even if one were to grant this statement, it would still be hard to understand the outpouring of violence that was used to eliminate both these enemies—a violence that far exceeded the prevailing guidelines of repression observed by any moderately civilized government.

One could listen to their arguments against Freud and Freudianism, classified as the chief enemies of Christian family life, a school dedicated to placing sex at the center of family life; and one might regard these arguments as antiquated, anti-scientific, obsolete. But what was the mechanism underlying those concepts that led to the kidnapping of the publisher of *Padres (Parents)*, a magazine devoted to modern parent-child relationships, and condemning the man to death? The campaign undertaken by my newspaper to save this journalist resulted in obtaining pardon for his life, but only on condition that he promise to suspend publication of his magazine and leave the country. He sent a message to me from abroad by secret emissary: "They told me I'd been saved by your campaign, but that you would not be saved."

While incarcerated in the clandestine prison known as Puesto Vasco, I was asked by an interrogator if I knew this journalist. The interrogator was proud of having tortured him. He spoke freely, knowing that he enjoyed impunity, convinced of his mission and never doubting that history would justify it. The psychological, ideological equation that animated Nazi officials in the concentration camps was being repeated.

Even the most irrational being finds it necessary to formulate a certain coherence around his irrationality in order to be able to maintain its continuity. The Argentine military tapped their vast reservoir of hatred and fantasy so as to synthesize their action into one basic concept: World War III had begun; the enemy was left-wing terrorism; and Argentina was the initial battleground chosen by the enemy.

Logically speaking, this simplified everything. The violence of repression was necessary inasmuch as Argentina had been chosen as the objective. Repression would be less if the

world would only understand the avant-garde role being performed by Argentina. But the world failed to understand
this, and certain democracies, as well as the Vatican, were
continually raising the issue of violation of human rights.
Furthermore, the Western press kept publishing reports on
these violations. The explanation for this stemmed from the
same mechanism, namely, the anti-Argentine campaign. So
we are presented with a coherent logic instead of the earlier
mere reincarnation of Nazi phobias:

1. World War III has broken out.

2. World War III is not a confrontation between democracies and communism, but between the entire world and
left-wing terrorism. This permits the maintenance of diplo-
matic relations with Communist countries and the acceptance of Russia as the principal partner in Argentine foreign
trade.

3. Argentina has been chosen as the battleground in the
initial phase of World War III.

4. Argentina is alone and misunderstood by those who
ought to be her natural allies, the Western democracies.
Hence, the unleashing of the anti-Argentine campaign.

Every week, in the clandestine prisons where I was held,
courses were given on World War III. These sessions went
under the rubric of the "Academy." They were generally
given by an army intelligence officer, and attendance was
obligatory for the entire staff of torturers, interrogators, and
kidnappers.

During these sessions the content of news articles was
often analyzed, and the conclusions that were reached—unbeknownst perhaps to the participants—invariably coincided with those of the members of the Nazi Party during the
early years of that organization. Corrupt Western democracy
was incapable of confronting the onslaught of communism;
Europe would go red; and only staunch Nazis could contain
the Communist power.

Following some of these sessions, my guards would be tempted by the possibility of talking to one of the chief perpetrators of this heinous plot to annihilate Argentina, certain aspects of which had just been analyzed in class. They'd come to the door of my cell and, through the crack sometimes, or by opening the door, they'd ask me questions, presumably to confirm what they'd just been taught. Once I briefed them on the Jewish lobby in the United States. They had to be taught how to spell "lobby" in English. Another time, I told them about the first Zionist Congress in Basel, and they wanted to know when a decision had been reached to have two Zionist states, one in Israel and one in Uganda, and why the idea of Uganda had then been abandoned in favor of Argentina.

Another day the "Academy" meeting took a dangerous turn. Simon Wiesenthal, the man who pursued Nazis, had divulged the existence of an important war criminal in Argentina, and Germany had requested his extradition. The Argentine government, ever eager to demonstrate publicly that it was not anti-Semitic—despite its failure to ban anti-Semitic violence among its security forces—consented to the extradition of the German subject, allowing him, however, to escape first to Paraguay. Those who attended the Academy in the clandestine prison where I was held felt that a true betrayal had taken place against their National Revolution. They all passed me by without saying a word, although at night they tied both my hands to the bars of the bed and left me there for twenty-four hours, something they hadn't done for a while.

What was the ideology of the armed forces? It could only be discerned through its activity, its repression, the world that it hated, but was hard to pinpoint in its public statements, which were impregnated with euphemisms and protocol denouncing official corruption and subversion and defending true democracy.

Naziism did not exist. There was no such thing as missing persons. Nor secret trials. Nor the death penalty.

Hate and ignorance. What you don't understand you destroy.
In his last book, *Night of the Aurochs,* unfinished when he
died, the American writer Dalton Trumbo has his central
character, a member of the SS, comment of the Jews: "I don't
understand these people; and, because I can't understand
them, I kill them."

While Trumbo was writing the book, he confided to a
friend: "The thing I seek to apprehend, the demon I'm trying
to capture, is the dark lust for power that all of us have, the
perversion of love as the inevitable consequence of power,
the delights of perversion when power becomes absolute,
and the grim conviction that in a period during which science has become enslaved by politics-cum-theology, all of
this can happen again."

9

For one month I've occupied a cell in the penal institute of the armed forces, situated about eighty kilometers from the city of Buenos Aires, in the section of Magdalena.

The military routine is strict. I'm in an isolation cell, given one hour of recreation a day, at which point I'm allowed to walk around the yard but not talk to other prisoners. When it rains, recreation is suspended. It is now winter, and when one of the three ward officers is on guard he orders recreation to take place very early in the morning so that we can't enjoy the sun, which reaches the yard around eleven. I receive visits on Saturdays and Sundays only from members of my immediate family. I'm allowed to take a hot bath three times a week, and meals are served four times a day.

As always, the problem is the toilet. This cell doesn't have one, and I must bang on the door whenever I need to go. One's needs, of course, are not conditioned by the guards' parsimony.

Everything conforms to the rules. I can read Spanish newspapers, but not the English-language paper published in Buenos Aires and sold legally on street newsstands. The officer's explanation is that every publication must pass censorship, and the censor is unable to read English. I tell him that if there were anything objectionable, the government wouldn't authorize publication of the newspaper. He's unauthorized to carry the dialogue so far.

I'm being detained in a military jail because I shall be appearing before a Special War Council, and must therefore spend a period of isolation in this institution. The Jewish New Year is approaching, and the Day of Atonement. My wife is requesting permission of the military tribunal for a rabbi to visit me: officially, there is freedom of worship in Argentina. The request goes unanswered, but both days the Catholic priest in the prison visits me in my cell.

The government modifies the Code of Military Justice before the trial is to begin; in other words, it changes the rules of the game after it's been determined that I'm to be examined before a military tribunal. Until now, an accused person could designate as his defense lawyer a military officer of any rank, either in active service or retired. A retired officer, whose career is over, has greater freedom of action; he isn't anticipating promotions. This clause is now modified, with the stipulation that the officer must be of lower rank than the president of the military tribunal. The president of the War Council that is to examine me is Colonel Clodoveo Battesti, hence my defense lawyer must hold a rank beneath that of colonel. Finally, I must select him from a list submitted to me by the War Council. I know no one on the list and am therefore choosing at random.

I had intended to designate as defense lawyer a personal friend, once president of the country, who I'm sure would have been unintimidated by threats. I must settle on a young officer whom I don't know but who's in active service, certainly aspiring to fresh promotions, and accustomed to receiving secret orders when necessary. In any event, to eliminate any doubts, he informs me at the interview in the military prison that this mission is an act of service. It's clear that if he'd had a choice, he would not have accepted, but he prepares conscientiously for the task of defending me. With respect to the torture I underwent and recount, he consoles me: these are errors committed in the course of an extremely difficult investigation. Yet I have the impression that, intellectually, he's attracted by the issue and will fight to defend me up to the limits of prudence dictated by "an act of service." I sense at least a desire on his part to understand every professional aspect of the function of a journalist. I have no illusions about the political dimension or the criminal brutality inflicted upon me during interrogations.

Those who knock on my door four times a day to deliver food are four young prisoners, deserters. Their jail sentences range from three to five years. Mornings, at dawn, they clean the ward, wash the meal utensils, and sing beautiful religious songs. They are Jehovah's Witnesses, a Christian sect whose young people refuse for conscientious reasons to serve in the armed forces. Although the Argentine constitution guarantees freedom of worship, the armed forces do not accept the principle of conscientious objection. As children, therefore, they're already aware that on reaching the age of eighteen, they will have to serve an extended period in prison. They don't escape, but accept the punishment as part of their religious faith. They are gentle and peaceful, and perform all the jobs and services in the prison.

They're aware that I'm incommunicado, and whenever they knock on my door and it's opened by the guard, they always find some way to exchange a few words. During the day, I wait for those four opportunities to talk to someone. And at night I recall the words they uttered, say them aloud, repeat them.

The guard understands the ruses they use to talk to me. But he feigns ignorance, though occasionally reprimanding them with a glance. They ask me if I have a plate. "Do you have a plate?" A few words. And I answer, "I do," making it a couple of words more. They tell me that the pizza is rather cold, and the soup better; or they'll add that it's a good idea for me to eat fish because it strengthens one's sight. Or they'll ask whether I want some more bread, or would like to sweep my cell, or was I given a towel? I've managed to hold dialogues of up to twelve words.

They are workers, peasants, day laborers, humble men. They advise me that there will be hot water at night, or predict that it will be less cold in the morning. They look for every conceivable way to convey to me that civilization has not come to an end, that I'm not the last remaining mortal enclosed in this cell, and that the possibility still exists of experiencing cordiality, camaraderie, solidarity, congeniality. Sometimes I have some chocolate, and the guard gives me permission to share it with them.

The headquarters of the Supreme Council of the Argentine armed forces is located in an old, rundown palace in the heart of Buenos Aires, about a thousand meters from the Government Building. I'd spent the night incommunicado at the central headquarters of the Federal Police in Buenos Aires, and was informed by those who transported me in a car trailed by two other cars that I would not be tied up, but that any wrong move on my part could mean my death sentence.

The military play military games; they love to imagine the danger of someone who presents no danger at all. Similar situations recurred time and again during my captivity. While I was under house arrest in my fifteenth-floor apartment, a police helicopter would often circle above the building, using its spotlights to illumine the room where I was enclosed. Once there was a light failure in my building, and within five minutes a military helicopter was hovering over the building and another opposite my room, illuminating it. They thought the Israeli army was about to launch an Entebbe-style operation to liberate me.

At the headquarters of the Armed Forces Supreme Council where Special War Council No. 2, which is going to examine me, is located, the military amuse themselves with all the attributes of protocol and the greatest possible imitation of legality. The seven members of the tribunal—three representatives from the army, two from the navy, and two from the air force—have all had in their possession for some time a copy of my statements, background on the case, presumed statements that I was forced to sign without having been able to read them first. From a reading of these documents, they concluded some time ago that it would be impossible to accuse me of any crime, and that after my interrogation the decision would be: lack of sufficient evidence for a trial.

Until the very moment of my appearance before the military court, I remained uninformed of the grounds for my arrest, the reasons, or even the accusations against me, if any existed. The court is simply to decide, after weighing the entire case, whether sufficient charges exist to justify a trial. But since they know in advance that no such charges do exist, they devote the day and a half allotted to my questioning to unleashing their ideology, neuroses, fantasies, hatreds, and phobias, and even manage to interject some amusing questions.

The protocol, of course, is strict. I mount the steep stairway, escorted by guards who hold my arms gently but firmly. At the top, I'm received by a uniformed army officer accompanied by two officers of lower rank. I'm invited, yes invited, to pass into a small office where I'm supposed to wait. Everything is correct and proper, though it's quite likely that these officers now offering me coffee are the very ones who were smiling in the clandestine prisons when I was jolted into the air by electric shocks while blindfolded.

The same officer takes me to the courtroom of the military tribunal where Special War Council No. 2 will be in session. It is an immense hall, about ten meters wide and twenty-five meters long. Dark, without windows, ancient, its walls covered with huge paintings that depict the great battles of Argentine independence, the conquest of the southern desert, and the war against the Indians. Dark boiserie, red curtains, high ceilings. I'm ordered to take a seat on a small,

round, backless red bench—the famous bench of the accused. I'm at a far end of the huge room. At the other end,
on a high dais, stands the crescent-shaped table of the military tribunal.

To my left is an army officer, the prosecuting attorney; to
my right, the defense attorney, also an army officer. He will
intercede only if an accusation is formulated; that is, if the
tribunal decides that the trial is to take place. Alongside me
is a small table with microphones. Behind, two young naval
officers serve as stenographers.

At a command, we all rise to our feet, and the members of
the tribunal enter through a side door. They walk slowly,
erect, firm of step. Uniformed, wearing caps, they climb the
dais, remain standing in front of their chairs until ordered by
the president of the tribunal to be seated. We all sit down.
They keep their caps on. The scene is imposing, the air spark-
ing with tension. We remain serious and silent.

The secretary of the tribunal, an army officer, reads the
data on me. I'm asked whether it's correct. I answer affirmatively. Only the president of the tribunal may speak; the
other members pass him the questions they wish to ask, written on slips of paper. Approximately every forty minutes, the
president interrupts the session and orders a five-minute
break. The sessions, in total, last about fourteen hours over
a period of two days. At each interruption, the entire ceremony is repeated: We rise to our feet, the members of the
tribunal retire; we rise to our feet, the members of the tribunal enter. The president asks: "Are you a Jew?"

Answer: "Yes, Mr. President."

A world of courts. And a world of the accused. Civil, military,
religious courts—everything has been judged, is judged, and
will be judged. And always, throughout history and the present, I've been among the accused. I never judged anyone,
and never shall.

At what point did I assume so much guilt? Or did I only

assume it when it was indicated that I was guilty? Is it thus a role assigned to me, this role of sinner, criminal, or simply culpable party—something that pride has obliged me to assume in order to convert it into a virtue? Have I assumed guilt merely for the potential, or mission, of transforming it into a virtue? Omnipotence? The sin of vanity? Or is it the temptation of delusion, employing a dynamic that converts Evil into Good? The exacerbation of Evil as a more immediate potential toward Good?

If you add up all the victims and victimizers, they form such a small percentage of the world population. What are the others engaged in? We victims and victimizers, we're part of the same humanity, colleagues in the same endeavor to prove the existence of ideologies, feelings, heroic deeds, religions, obsessions. And the rest of humanity, the great majority, what are they engaged in?

On that day in September 1977, how many of us in the whole world were seated upon the accused man's bench? How many were judged for what they did? How many were judged for having been born? The war against Naziism had ended thirty-two years and four months before, the Nazi criminals have been tried and sentenced, anti-Semitism has been defined, concretized, pinpointed, and cured. And yet, these same thirty-two years and four months later, in the city of Buenos Aires, I continued to be a citizen under total suspicion, proven to have been born on the wrong, absurd side of humanity; involved, due to birth and stupidity, or perhaps sheer inclination, in the treacheries under judgment into which I had relapsed. But judged by whom? And when? In which remote corner of Spain, Germany, France, Poland, Russia, or Syria? In different countries, at different superimposed junctures, in repeated countries and repeatedly, with cumulative and repetitive accusations, always to return to the same place, mine, yet unacceptable because it's intolerable: I was born a Jew.

I was not born a Zionist, the accusation usually paired with that initial suspicion of one's birth.

Nor was I born a dissident, a seemingly inevitable derivation of birth.

Nor was I born a young leftist, a defender of prisoners, an activist in organizations for the defense of human rights.

The biological consequences of original sin—the birth of an individual born a Jew.

And yet there's someone at this moment seated on a backless red bench, fifty centimeters high, in Cuba, and he isn't a Jew. What becomes intolerable is the notion that perhaps there are no Others, that the Other doesn't exist. But there may be someone in Czechoslovakia seated on a chair, if not a bench, in front of an ordinary table, if not a dais, someone who isn't a Jew; and the existence of that Other is what makes my fate seem open still to appeal.

In this world of tribunals and of the accused, I search fervently for the relief that should be forthcoming from the Other, if truly we belong to that vast little group of victims. But once again I find only consolation, not identity. I find the consolation of solidarity, but not that of inevitability, for though we share the same aspirations, his guilt is not inevitable, and he will always be lacking the guilt needed to reach me. And if he is unable to reach me, it means that I am united with him, but not he with me. Not in the fullness of my guilt, which I possess in its totality, but which he possesses only in part.

There will always be a place where I'm alone, totally alone before my judges, who are also his judges, and before whom I appear in his company, but suddenly abandoned by him in that singular, inevitable, incomparable, dark, and superb solitude that always begins with the same ritual: "Are you a Jew?"

"Are you a Jew?"
"Yes, Mr. President."
"Your partners, are they or were they Jews?"
"Yes, Mr. President."

"Are you a Zionist?"

"Yes, Mr. President."

"Are your partners always Zionists?"

"No, Mr. President."

"When did your Zionist activities begin?"

"At the age of eight, Mr. President. My mother enrolled me in a sports club called Macabi."

"Did your mother take you or did you go by yourself?"

"My mother took me, Mr. President."

"Therefore, one could say that it wasn't a voluntary act on your part."

"I was taken by my mother, Mr. President."

"In what way did your Zionist activities continue?"

"While attending high school, I was invited to participate in a student Zionist group called Avuca. I was fourteen years old."

"Does 'Avuca' mean 'torch'?"

"Yes, Mr. President."

"Which means we could say that at age fourteen you voluntarily began your Zionist activities in Argentina?"

"Yes, Mr. President."

"What did you do?"

"We met on Saturdays, Mr. President, in the basement of the Argentine Zionist Federation. We had a library, a Ping-Pong table, and several chess sets. We were all Jewish high-school students."

"Were you being indoctrinated?"

"Every Saturday, a member of the University Zionist Atheneum, which operated on the top floors, presented a talk on Zionism or Jewish history."

I was fourteen years old, went to school mornings, and afternoons worked as a messenger for a jewelry store. We lived in the heart of the Jewish quarter. My father had died two years before. My mother worked as a street vendor, my brother studied and helped her. On Saturday mornings we

had to attend classes, but in the afternoon the jewelry store
was closed. After lunch, my chores were to wash the dishes
and pots, iron my shirts, and scrub the stairway of the building. In exchange for running this small apartment building
in the Jewish quarter where each family occupied a single
room, we were given a free room. For this, we had to scrub
the bathrooms, corridors, stairways, and collect the rents. My
mother paid me ten cents for washing the stairways, the
price of a chocolate bar, and instructed me to buy it shortly
before the Avuca activities were over so that I could save her
a piece. In the winter, I had to hurry to get to the municipal
bathhouse where there was hot water so as to return and get
dressed in time and not miss any of the Avuca activities.

Ping-Pong and chess were novelties. Zionism and Jewish
history, true discoveries. But meeting Jewish adolescents
who didn't work, were well-to-do, dressed in suits, and had
money, this was mind-boggling.

There were also young people of sixteen and seventeen.
And they were the ones responsible for the abrupt end of my
childhood, thrusting me headlong into the world I would
never thereafter abandon. Emilio Salgari and Alexander
Dumas had to be set aside in order to read Jack London,
Upton Sinclair, John Dos Passos, Henri Barbusse, and Erich
Maria Remarque. On May 1, you had to join the great Socialist demonstration supporting the defense of Madrid, and
carry overhead the blue-and-white flag with the star of David
amid that sea of red flags. In that year of 1937, you had to
explain that Zionism was a national liberation movement
and that involvement in Zionism provided a kind of additional energy for the international struggle against fascism,
Franco, Hitler, and Mussolini. In small groups, you had to
cover the streets of the Jewish quarter, the Once District,
where we lived and had our headquarters, to be on the look-
out for Fascist, anti-Semitic groups who defaced the walls of
synagogues and schools, scribbling SERVE YOUR COUNTRY,
KILL A JEW, or improvising little grandstands in front of Jewish cafés where they launched their harangues against those

very Jews. There we were, with our heavy Ping-Pong rackets, made of wood in those days, flinging ourselves against the Fascists until two or three bored policemen would separate us and lead a few Jewish youths off to the nearby police station.

I still remember, at age fourteen, standing in front of that police station, crying because my brother had been kicked inside following one of those skirmishes. And I recall my mother, right there, summoned by friends, explaining in her faltering Spanish that her Yosele was only trying to prevent some Jews from being beaten up, and that she was sure the police chief was a good Christian and against fights that were started in the quarter by hooligans who came from outside.

There, at Avuca, when I was already fifteen, two good-looking young men arrived whom we'd never seen, handsome in their white shirts with military pockets and blue kerchief at the neck, to inform us that they were Jewish Boy Scouts in addition to being Socialist Zionists; and that we ought to learn about scouting so as to reacquaint ourselves with the land we'd left so many centuries ago. We ought to return to the land, to Israel, which was ours and under socialism, for the nation we wanted to build had to be the synthesis of the dreams of prophets past and present, namely, humanist socialism. There, in Argentina, stood those two young men from Hashomer Hatzair, and there at Avuca on that memorable night when I heard them speak I became destined for that world I would never abandon and never try to abandon —a world that at times took the form of Zionism, at times the struggle for human rights, at times the fight for freedom of expression, and at other times again the solidarity with dissidents against all totalitarianisms. And it was that world, unique in its beauty and martyrdom, that mythology of pain and memory, that cosmic vision imbued with nostalgia and the future, that Jewish mother charged with hope, resignation, and magic . . . it was all of that world that Colonel Clodoveo Battesti, president of the Argentine military tribu-

nal and head of Special War Council No. 2, sought to understand.

He wanted me to confess. To convert that whole consum-
ing mission of love and destiny, identity and future, into a
confession.

"Did you at any point abandon Zionism?"

"No, Mr. President."

"Yet, according to this police report, in 1944 you were
arrested for belonging to an organization affiliated with the
Communist Party."

"I was arrested in 1944, Mr. President, while attending a
film festival of the Argentine League for Human Rights. I was
in jail for only twenty-four hours because it was proven that
I hadn't participated in that organization, which the police
considered Communist."

"During that period, you belonged to the Youth League
for Freedom, which was also registered as an affiliate organization of the Communist Party."

"That's true, I did belong to that organization. The members were young supporters of an Allied victory during
World War II. They disseminated news on the fighting being
waged by Great Britain, China, the United States, Russia, and
France, without discrimination shown toward any of these
countries. They also took up collections for the purchase of
medicines that were sent to the Allied nations. What other
organization, Mr. President, could I possibly have belonged
to?"

"*I* didn't belong to that organization."

"Mr. President, can you imagine a young Jew in 1944
fighting for a Nazi victory?"

"That organization was dissolved by the police for being
considered Communist."

"That designation was the police's. I belonged to it as an
anti-Fascist, a Jew, and a Zionist. Mr. President, in view of the
evident interest regarding my relationship with Zionism,

I think I ought to explain to the court the meaning of Zionism."

"We're well aware of the nature of Zionism. Confine yourself to answering the questions."

In 1939 we had no radio, but early in the morning, when the sirens of the three big newspapers in Buenos Aires went off, my mother hurried out into the street and came back with the news that France and England had declared war on Hitler. She was radiant. "In one month he'll be defeated. Our brothers will be avenged."

In 1940 and 1941, veterans of the Spanish Civil War began arriving in Argentina, traveling in small groups, from the Far East, the north, and Africa. I couldn't tear myself away from the bars where they congregated, held their conversations, lived their bohemian lives, their unique, romantic postwar lives. For the first time I heard about the betrayal of democracies from men who'd sought to combat fascism. I heard about the Russian intrigues, the massacre of Trotskyites and anarchists, about the real names of the heroes who had become legendary to me and the young members of our Hashomer Hatzair group when we attended solidarity meetings for Republican Spain—mournful, heroic Spain—when we learned the poems of Pablo Neruda, Louis Aragon, Paul Éluard, and Stephen Spender, and were stirred by Upton Sinclair's *They Shall Not Pass* and Ilya Ehrenburg's articles.

We were eighteen, nineteen, and twenty years old at the time, clustered around those men who had had firsthand contact with fascism and explained battle strategy to us, men absorbed in their war, that genuine war; and we acquired words and techniques in order to understand, to attempt to understand the successive Allied defeats, convinced that fascism would be defeated.

Those adolescent youthful convictions! We'd chosen that moment to prepare a group of young Jews for work on the land, collective work, for who could doubt that the war would be won, a Zionist-Socialist state established, and that all of us would be going to kibbutzim? In those years of 1943 and 1944, I too learned how to plow the earth, to milk cows, to plant seeds. Yet my blood and imagination were engaged in the struggle against fascism, though there was little I could do other than sign manifestos, obtain signatures for manifestos, collect money, buy medicines, and roll bandages.

Rolling bandages! I remember my mother going every night to solidarity committee meetings at the Victory League and leaning over a table to roll bandages, after having attended that day to breakfast, making our room, going out to sell clothes, coming back to fix lunch, going out again to sell clothes, doing the shopping, fixing dinner, then rolling bandages. Sometimes she took with her to those neighborhood committee meetings a little blue-and-white collection box from Keren Kayemet (the Jewish National Fund) to collect some coins for land purchase in Israel, although she never mustered enough Spanish to explain the intricate truth about Zionism or why buying land in Israel need be a priority at a time when mankind's destiny was unfolding in Stalingrad. An educated Jewish woman asserted that this was not the proper moment—the fighting was not in Palestine, the Nazis were elsewhere—but my mother persisted, and, resorting no longer to arguments but merely to a plea for solidarity, managed to collect a few coins owing to the inevitable community of feeling that wells up amongst women.

Little did my mother realize that her son, at that very moment, was brokenhearted because, at twenty, he was engaged in ideological, political, and philosophical debates while the fighting was going on in Stalingrad, and the names of the various kibbutzim seemed so remote, indecipherable, and unpronounceable.

Yes, I did belong to the Youth League for Freedom, because it was impossible to go to Palestine or to war. Because, at age twenty, in 1943, not to fight against fascism was utterly intolerable, and yet all that one could ever do was collect money, roll bandages, sign manifestos, and try to prove to everyone that Zionism wasn't the obsession of a small group, a hitherto unknown illness, the derivative of North American monopolies and armament dealers. Being able to fight would have simplified everything.

At the Free French Committee, I was told that only Frenchmen or the sons of Frenchmen were being accepted, for there was an excess of volunteers and limited possibilities of transferring them all to Europe or North Africa. At the British Embassy, I was welcomed as a volunteer because of my willingness to go to Asia, but when my application was filed, revealing my Russian origin, this proved counter to an existing agreement with the USSR prohibiting contingents with "White Russians." At the United States Embassy, I was told that no volunteers were being accepted. That morning, at noon, on leaving the U.S. Embassy, which was only two hundred meters from the Government Building, I witnessed the peaceful takeover of the Government Building by the Argentine army. It was June 4, 1943, and Colonel Juan Domingo Perón made his appearance, still privately and confidentially, but already spinning the threads of military conspiracy on the Argentine political scene.

There was confusion at the venerable Plaza de Mayo facing the Government Building, and amid this confusion I organized a group of young people who were shouting anti-Fascist slogans and heading toward the headquarters of *El Pampero*, the Nazi newspaper financed by the German Embassy. The police guarding the building prevented us from burning it, and I spent that night in jail, my ankles beaten by a guard.

From that day on, the years of my youth would be further complicated, for all my time, energy, reading, studies, and knowledge flowed in countless directions. And these directions, in my mind totally connected and integrated, seemed so contradictory in the eyes of others, and were so hard to explain: We were fighting against Perón's dictatorship and his friendship with fascism; we were fighting for Zionism, and we needed to absorb the classical writers; we were siding with the Allies but were opposed to England in Palestine; we were pro-Russia in Stalingrad but anti-Russian with respect to their behavior in Spain and their anti-Zionism. We were trying to establish a parallel between Marx and Freud, Picasso and Socialist realism; we were the unlikely disciples of Ehrenburg's Julio Jurenito, but announced without any confusion and a touch of solemnity that when the war was over, the Allies ought to grant independence to all their colonies since this was why fascism had been defeated. And we were demanding a second front while remaining staunchly united with Republican Spain, whose struggle against fascism provided our first taste of anti-fascism, as savored in those long conversations in Buenos Aires cafés like the House of Troy with refugee commanders of the Brigades, the Fifth, those from Miaja, Madrid, Asturias, Teruel, and Málaga. . . .

And now that vast sea of doubts and imagination, youth and dreams, that miraculous coexistence of world suffering and Jewish suffering, that anti-Fascist solidarity, that anti-totalitarian dream of my youth, was being suddenly reduced to a police report flourished by Army Colonel Clodoveo Battesti, president of Special War Council No. 2. Colonel Battesti claimed that he was perfectly aware of what Zionism was and didn't need to have it explained by someone for whom such awful and futile tragedy had created personal doubts regarding Zionism and the Jewish people. Colonel Battesti wanted things to be summed up in a tidy, clear-cut manner, uncluttered for the mind of an Argentine officer by the individual doubts of someone who responded to the news and pictures of Auschwitz, Warsaw, and Babi Yar with questions about himself and all mankind.

Colonel Battesti would have had an easier time understanding Nazi statistics, which computed everything. And Nazi philosophy, too, where hatred figured prominently and love was easily identifiable—hatred of the Jew and love of the Fatherland. Jacobo Timerman, on the other hand, needed to explain what he was doing in the Youth League for Freedom, why he was supporting that strange alliance between the

United States and Russia, why he was active in Zionism and simultaneously reading Freud and fighting against Perón, and was also a Socialist though claiming to be opposed to Russian totalitarianism. Then, subsequently, as newspaper publisher and a powerful, well-to-do man, appealing for habeas corpus on behalf of a missing guerrilla fighter. This was the same individual who, according to the police report, had given a lecture at the age of twenty or twenty-two at the Academy of Plastic Arts, formulating a proposal in support of cubism, structuralism, constructivism, or some other ism.

Nothing matched in Jacobo Timerman's replies, whereas Colonel Clodoveo Battesti's questions during these proceedings held by the Argentine armed forces at Special War Council No. 2 seemed so very neat and precise.

"Did you have any contact with the terrorists?"

"No, Mr. President."

"But you knew terrorists, didn't you?"

"Mr. President, some of the people classified as terrorists by the armed forces were members of the Argentine Parliament. I had conversations with them in their role as legislators, as I might with any other legislator. I also had conversations with the military commandants of the three branches of the armed services. This was normal for a newspaper publisher."

"Timerman, answer the questions. You remind me of a pickpocket claiming innocence because the number of handbags that he didn't steal was greater than those he did. Did you have any contact with the terrorists, yes or no?"

"No, Mr. President."

"Yet the declarations of leading terrorists often appeared in your newspaper. How did these declarations fall into your hands?"

"Mr. President, I never printed declarations of clandestine individuals. How could I classify as terrorist a person who called a press conference, hadn't been arrested by the police

or armed forces, and whose statements were broadcast on
state television? All the newspapers printed such statements,
yet their publishers are not in front of this War Council."

"Still, when one of those terrorists was arrested, you involved yourself conspicuously in the case."

"If he was given judicial access, I did not deal with it
conspicuously. Only when this was denied did I feel that the
issue of legal deprivation was at stake and affected the nation's judicial structure."

"And, incidentally, you were doing the terrorists a fav-
or. . . ."

"The country, Mr. President. Anyhow, I'd like to mention
that I was the only newspaper publisher who personally
signed articles condemning terrorism and accusing terrorist
leaders, by name, of specific crimes."

"Some people say you did this to conceal your true activities."

"That's a childish statement, Mr. President."

"You're here to answer questions, not give opinions."

At a certain historical moment, in a specific geographic
place, there are attitudes that are contrary to the nature of
things. Why should a professionally competent, informed,
and educated journalist have assumed that it was possible in
the struggle against left-wing and right-wing terrorism to
maintain an independent position, opposed to both and favorable to democracy?

In Argentina, everyone not directly involved in the struggle was engaged in survival. The political parties, especially;
and certainly newspapers. Why should someone who wasn't
attempting to survive fail to arouse suspicion? On more than
one occasion, the Minister of the Interior assured me that
there would be no conflicts between me and the military
government if I ceased printing appeals for habeas corpus.
With the exception of the Buenos Aires *Herald*, every newspaper had by now ceased doing this. It was an easy decision

to make, yet impossible. Almost a desirable decision, yet impossible. Printing the appeals for habeas corpus that relatives of the disappeared presented to the courts for information on sons, husbands, and wives was seldom fruitful. Still, the faces of relatives that appeared at *La Opinión,* plus the absurd conviction that it was possible to recover a human being, plus the need to believe that a newspaper constitutes a powerful institution, precluded any position other than printing those appeals. Otherwise, one would have simply had to tell these people to forget about it, to accept death, that no one could do a thing, and that they should pray. But this was what religion told them. Or, perhaps, to tell them to be patient, which was what politicians told them. Or to tell them that it was best not to create a scandal, for that meant a death sentence, which was what the police told them. Or not to receive them, which was the policy of the other newspapers. Thus, the only remaining alternative was to receive them, print what had to be printed, inform them that instances had occurred of missing people reappearing and that they ought to keep fighting. Or else close down the newspaper.

The one thing that proved impossible was to shut your eyes.

More than once my staff and I considered temporary suspension of publication. Or for me and my family perhaps to leave the country, while the staff would gradually modify the nature of the newspaper, converting *La Opinión* into a more-or-less acceptable vehicle.

I toyed with these easy, sensible, accessible, soothing notions. To sit down with the Minister of the Interior for coffee with a sense of immunity to danger; to close the newspaper for a while and forget about the daily desperation and that sense of impotence; to go abroad and allow the newspaper to undergo normalization, "naturalization," adjusting to the naturalness of things. To desist from that vain battle, or that vanity of striving for principles which could only serve as examples, for in fact they had no practical ends. It would all have been so easy, and was so tempting.

How could a military tribunal comprehend these doubts and fears? How could a military tribunal, a military government, conceive of someone feeling an obligation, the force of an idea, the inevitability of a conviction? How could the Argentine military government of 1976–77 accept the fact that a Jew would sacrifice his economic welfare, his tranquility, for an idea, unless that idea represented some illegitimate agreement, something as unnatural and illegitimate as his own birth, the unnatural circumstances of being a Jew?

But even earlier, in 1973, when Perónism came to power, during those early months of Hector Campora's presidency and the decisive influence of the Montoneros guerrilla groups, how could the Left conceive of a Jew sacrificing his tranquility and income, risking his life to discuss with them their ideology, calling them the lunatic Left, Fascists of the Left, and denouncing their ideas?

This was utterly suspicious to the extreme Left, the Montoneros, and equally so to the military government.

What relationship was there between *La Opinión*'s rational approach to Argentine life and the Argentine reality of those years? What were its strategy, motivation, goals, and mandates?

In looking for an explanation that went beyond the unacceptable notions of democracy, freedom, tolerance, and coexistence, both Left and Right were bound to concur at some point. There had to be some imposed mandate that *La Opinión* was obeying. The newspaper was obviously not freely electing daily suicide, a dubious flirtation with death.

Hence *La Opinión* was an adversary of the Left for being Zionist, an adversary of the military government for being terrorist, an adversary of mass culture for publishing sophisticated writers, an adversary of Christian morality for publishing leftist writers, an adversary of the Left for publishing Soviet dissidents, and an adversary of the family for publishing in its Science Section an article on the sexual habits of young Americans. *La Opinión* was a supporter of terrorism in opposing a break of relations with Cuba, claiming that this was disadvantageous to Argentina's international policy; yet it was an adversary of the Left for admonishing Cuba to abandon its policy of exporting revolution and providing both haven and training to terrorists who had escaped from their own countries.

La Opinión, in those years, was opposed to the natural order of things and refused to accept waiting patiently for that order to be modified, without intervening. It was this continual intervention at every level of life, incurring every risk, probing into the most confidential areas, that made *La Opinión* a suspect entity, for neither of the two sectors could understand what benefit was in store for the newspaper. And it was hard to acknowledge that there was none. This quest for the potential benefit to that Jew, to that impertinent newspaper, to that declared Zionist, that omnipotent journalist, this quest for the underlying motives behind such irresponsibility, lunacy, audacity, or manifest destiny, was pursued in Argentina by military courts, civil courts, secret terrorist tribunals, politicians, journalists, Jewish community leaders, and Zionist leaders.

In everyone's eyes, something inexplicable and suspicious was going on, and there had to be an explanation. In that world of unceasing pathological obsession, who could acknowledge the existence of a limited group of people at *La Opinión,* the Buenos Aires *Herald,* and the Permanent Assembly of Human Rights adhering to some of the simplest verities and sentiments, which they refused to discard and which were stronger than fear? Sentiments that prompted certain Christian priests and rabbis, though terrified, to visit prisoners in jails and to search for missing people; that prompted certain lawyers to agree to serve as legal counsel to the families of those who'd disappeared; and certain journalists to publish articles and pray silently that the newspaper might suspend publication before the article left the printing press with their signatures at the bottom.

How was one to encompass all of this, those dreams of freedom of the press, of democracy and coexistence, of tolerance and liberty? How was one to encapsulate it into the replies given to Colonel Clodoveo Battesti, president of Special War Council No. 2, who upon fulfillment of his high judicial military mission would be appointed executive head of a state television channel wherein life is seen to unfold with infinite humor, grace, beauty, spontaneity, and ease?

In short, what is there to explain? To Colonel Battesti, nothing. But how to explain to myself those scores and hundreds of articles appealing for mercy for a kidnapped soldier, a missing terrorist, pleading for the lives of the very individuals who wanted to put an end to my own?

Do I not, I ask myself, wind up being suspect in my own eyes for having undertaken that impossible choice, that permanent vigil of my own despair, experiencing a kind of omnipotence in being the victim? The Victim. Didn't that hatred of all those who'd caused me to surrender the best of myself, my courage and sacrifice, didn't that hatred wind up asserting itself within my fear, leading me at times to believe that perhaps there was indeed some underlying motive, something that had escaped me—some vague guilt hidden behind my principles, my intrusive honesty, my inexplicable humanitarian mission?

At times I felt like those Jews who wound up being convinced by the Nazis that they were objects of hatred because they were intrinsically hateful objects. At times my hatred became so intolerable that it resembled their need to hate, and even obeyed the logic of their hatred. I was torn by painful fantasies about humanity's survival and the futility of that survival, while at the same time I'd be sending an open letter to the Argentine president pleading for the life of a missing Uruguayan politician or attempting to explain to the lunatic fringe of the Left that terrorism was alienating the Left from the people, that the people aspired to political struggle rather than terrorism.

This whole oppressive universe toppling over me and bearing down on my anguish like a gravestone had to be encompassed within a single coherent reply to Colonel Clodoveo Battesti, who a few months after presiding over this court-martial would be devoting himself to decisions as to which chorus singers to use on the next Channel 9 show on Buenos Aires television.

The members of the War Council, in the course of that fourteen-hour session, traced my entire life—or my presumed life as it emerged in the police reports accumulated under my name during my thirty-year span as a political journalist. That mentality, formed in military institutes which imbue the armed forces with its messianic sense, had already categorized me as a criminal by birth, although they'd unearthed no plausible crime that lent itself to publication under banner headlines in Argentine newspapers eager to prove that my kind of journalism was a romantic, childish fantasy leading only to disaster.

That totalitarian mentality—proud to have at its mercy this impertinent intellectual, this leftist Zionist, this dreamy adolescent poet—found logical, coherent questions to reveal the high index of my criminality. Their legal adviser, however, a military attorney who'd made his way through university classrooms that were contemptuous of civilians and opposed them as a race, this uniformed attorney advised the court not to press charges that weren't clearly specified in the anti-subversive laws or the Code of Military Justice.

The War Council, from the onset of its investigation, realized that the anti-Vietnamese War campaign could not be classified as a criminal act. But still, how could Colonel Clodoveo Battesti refrain from alluding to certain articles in *La Opinión* as constituting part of the anti-U.S.A. Communist conspiracy?

No normally acceptable or interpretable code would claim that an article in support of a firm U.S. policy toward General Pinochet, the right-wing leader of Chile, was part of a Marxist-Zionist conspiracy jointly plotted with Washington liberals against Latin American Christian governments. Yet, how

128 PRISONER WITHOUT A NAME

could these self-serving officers refrain from the temptation of forcing me to explain those articles, that political line, that alternate support and criticism of the United States? How could they fail to discover in those conflicting aspects of international fact some satanic combination of forces merging in this Jewish Zionist, leftist, arrogant, suicidal journalist?

Special War Council No. 2 ruled that there was no existing charge against the aforesaid Jacobo Timerman, that he remained therefore outside their jurisdiction, and that there were no existing grounds for holding him under arrest. This occurred in late September 1977, and was communicated to me on October 13, 1977.

The interrogations, declarations, and explanations were over. But the government of the armed forces kept me under house arrest two years longer, until September 24, 1979, when for the second time the Supreme Court of Justice declared that it found no grounds for my continued arrest. How could the Supreme Court appraise the army's conviction that Jacobo Timerman was the Antichrist despite the fact that this was impossible to prove? The Minister of the Interior stated that he was convinced Timerman was a subversive, but had unfortunately been unable to prove it. The army generals met and voted by a broad majority, despite the Supreme Court's ruling, that the accused Timerman ought to remain imprisoned, preferably in a military garrison, and furthermore, that the Supreme Court ought to resign. Only when President Jorge Rafael Videla, under international pressure, threatened to quit if the Supreme Court's order to release Timerman was not respected, did the army come up with a Solomon-like solution (unaware, perhaps, that Solomon was a Jewish king): it annulled Timerman's Argentine citizenship, expelled him from the country, and confiscated his goods, without heeding the release order that had been given a second time by the Supreme Court.

Need one add that Argentine newspapers, jurists, political

friends of the government, Jewish community leaders—all those who will one day claim they knew nothing, like the Germans who claimed total unawareness of the existence of concentration camps—congratulated the government for obeying a court ruling and faithfully respecting the majesty of Justice?

10

Some ideologues of the Argentine military dictatorship felt that the best means of explaining their own motives and actions was by trying to define the dangers facing Argentina. This method of explaining a goal not by what one desires to obtain or accomplish but by what one desires to avoid is typical of the left-wing and right-wing totalitarian mentalities whose terrorist violence broke out in Argentina. They could never explain what it was that they wished to construct, but were always categorical in terms of what they wished to annihilate.

One of the most elaborate definitions went as follows: "Argentina has three main enemies: Karl Marx, because he tried to destroy the Christian concept of society; Sigmund Freud, because he tried to destroy the Christian concept of the family; and Albert Einstein, because he tried to destroy the Christian concept of time and space."

For any moderately civilized individual, this statement reveals a clear desire to revert to the society of the Middle Ages. It is a form of rejection of modern society, and of attempts to understand the contradictions of the contemporary age. For a totalitarian mind, there are no existing contradictions to justify a pluralist, tolerant society. Nothing exists but enemies or friends.

For a Jew, the description put forth by a military ideologue as to the nature of Argentina's main enemies is like the appearance of an ancient ghost, since the figures chosen to illustrate the enemy are three Jews. True, one of the most virulent anti-Semitic tracts was written by Marx himself in his book *The Jewish Question*. But whereas some fairly civilized Communists feel that this book contains certain erroneous evaluations and must be analyzed in light of the problems of the period when it was written, a right-wing totalitarian sees it merely as proof that Jews sometimes employ contradictory methods to confuse non-Jews and to make them believe that the Jews are divided.

Some Argentine military sectors do not concur with this argument, but will never admit it for fear they might appear pro-Jewish. Indeed, at various times, they've voiced the need to avoid any expression of anti-Semitism, maintaining this as a tactical necessity, however, rather than an ideological position or an expression of principle. Their main argument in favor of avoidance of any suspicion of anti-Semitism invariably has been the need to avoid confrontation with the powerful Jewish community in the United States. These sectors have always been obliged to act with special care to forestall being accused of "weakness before the enemy," one of the chief anathemas that can befall an Argentine military man, particularly if it stems from his own ranks.

This group of moderates was largely counterbalanced by the extreme wing of the armed forces, and the policy of repression and extermination during the first four years of the military dictatorship was in the hands of this sector. Its adherents hung pictures of Hitler in the rooms where Jewish political prisoners were interrogated; special tortures were invented for Jewish prisoners; the food allotment to Jewish prisoners in clandestine prisons was reduced; rabbis who dared to go to the jails to visit Jewish prisoners were humiliated. And, basically, the extremists encouraged and protected books and magazines that contained anti-Semitic literature. Some magazines pronounced that President Jimmy Carter was a Jew and that his real name was Braunstein with the same blend of levity, hatred, and rationalizations used by the Nazis in their claim that Franklin Roosevelt was a Jew.

This book . . . It's painful . . . Most of the time I feel paralyzed. I cannot prevent the memories of the tortures from spreading themselves over my daily life, over the long hours that make up a daily life—like a jigsaw puzzle that a neat and careful child spreads piece by piece over the floor of his room. The scenes of beatings, electric shocks, solitary confinement, cold baths in winter, combine themselves into the final image, and the result is always the same: the shout with which my interrogators used to insult me when they were really furious—Jew!

I try to remake my life, those long empty spaces of daily life, and I spread the pieces out again. I remake the puzzle with new scenes, small new figures, bits I lift out of places close by, from two years, three years ago. And again the result is the insult they shouted with utter pleasure, enjoying it—Jew!

Again and again the Jew returns to history; to my personal anecdote and to all of history. In the decade of the seventies, in a remote country, the southernmost of all countries, in a nation just 160 years old, in that far country torn by a war between Right and Left, all those who kill push the Jew into the present, and into history. And during those years I saw the Jew trying to understand, to escape, to survive, to hide, to convince, to ask for forgiveness.

In the decade of the seventies, in a remote country, I saw repeated, promoted, and exploited the scandal of the political Jew, the economic Jew, the journalist Jew, the subversive Jew—with words and ideas that translated into Spanish of the 1970s the same ideas of the corrupt Jew, the erotic Jew, the lying Jew, the cowardly Jew, the traitorous Jew as were expressed in German in the 1930s and 1940s.

Either the Right or the Left could have arrested me, or kidnapped or murdered me, in that country, so young and far away, because they both had sufficient motive. I was the kind of journalist they didn't need to force into history; I entered willingly. No one had to impose my enemies on me. I selected them myself. I didn't avoid them: I pointed them out, marked them, attacked them.

Why then, in that arrogant journalist, that aggressive accuser of Right and Left, did they single out the Jewish aspect as the most dangerous, which must be eliminated?

In that world of political conspiracies, ideological alliances, dialectical adventures, why did they accuse the Jew, torture the Zionist, select the "Jewish conspiracy" as the most hated object?

I know the Argentine political situation, and I know that the army officers did not need to involve the Jew, even for strategic reasons, as a scapegoat. So the gratuitousness of the act frightens me, that is, the existence of a hatred so pure, so unreal, without cause and without object, without end, eternal.

Perhaps Hitler did the same, selecting the "Jewish conspiracy" as the major one among all those he could have chosen, and carrying the results of his hatred to its limits. But it is precisely that which is so frightening. The fact that those actions, which can still be seen and heard with such clarity after scarcely thirty-five years, should be yearned for, dreamed of, sought after by the Argentine military in the 1970s.

It is frightening to have discovered, in those long sessions of torture in the clandestine military prisons of Argentina, that what seemed unthinkable is thought; that the words which seemed unrepeatable are repeated; and that the silences which were incomprehensible, the passivity or indifference, are now explained and justified.

And it frightens me to think that we are all the same. That

in a given moment, we Jews all become Jews again, only Jews. That a Jew is only that, a Jew. And that the others are not Jews. And really, they are not.

And above all, it frightens me that everything I am saying has already been said. That it has even been explained. Moreover, that all the possible answers have been catalogued and computed. And I suppose that I understand most of them. However, here I am, with all this having happened in my own life, and I don't know what to do because I am paralyzed. It seems impossible that it has happened. Indeed, what seems impossible is that it all has been repeated.

Admittedly, it has not been repeated with the same magnitude. But does the key to it all lie in the scale? It is true that it has not been taken to the same limits, to the same competent manufacture of hatred. But is it possible that the key is to be found in the capacity, the systematization, the style?

I think that the key lies in the character of the hatred, its motive, its object. And it is that which has been repeated, returning like a perfect mummy that begins to walk, and offering us again its symbols, its magic, its excitement from other times.

Isn't this frightening enough? Then let's think that once again, after the hatred is repeated, so is the silence, the complicity of those who could have prevented it. Because there is another key: it could have been prevented. The degree of solidarity with the victims does not matter, because it is simply part of the human condition. What is important is that the crimes could have been prevented, and that is a sin of our historic condition.

What is frightening is to realize how content we feel because we suppose there are deeds that cannot be repeated. It is true that 6 million European Jews cannot be murdered; tortured and murdered. But if, only thirty-five years after this did happen, the Jew can be considered the enemy, tortured and killed for being that enemy, then he has kept his place in history, his historic condition persists. And his helplessness to change his relationship with history persists, as does the world's inability to help him or understand him.

We were not all Jews in those hidden prisons. Many of us were. We Jews continued to be Jews, and being Jewish was a category of guilt, even when we were declared innocent of other offenses and absolved of other crimes.

I believe that all this could have been prevented. By the Jews themselves, by the Christians. But it was not. And remembering what happened in Europe, uniting the two experiences, the German one of the 1930s and the Argentine one of the 1970s, it is difficult to find consolation. There is no possible consolation.

In the clandestine prisons, and then in the official prisons of Argentina, they pounded it into my skin, my head, my bones: We Jews still occupy the same place in history. We have that place reserved.

The only thing we cannot guess is the magnitude that place will have, nor the moment we will be pushed into it. What is the magnitude of what happened in Argentina? Was it really important? Most of those killed were not Jews, and if we continue to feel sorry for ourselves as Jews, we will end up being hated by the non-Jewish victims, by the families of those priests and nuns who were murdered, by the parents of those missing boys and girls who were raised in the Christian faith. But in the solitude of prison, it is so sad to be beaten for being Jewish. There is such despair when they torture you for being Jewish. It seems so humiliating to have been born.

Anti-Semitism has always existed in Argentina, as in so many countries of the world. In the most democratic of countries, in one way or another, the Jew who enters into a relationship with his society—especially in politics and journalism—feels his condition as a Jew in reference to others more than in relation to himself. Others point it out to him if he —as a humanist, a freethinker, a liberal—has forgotten it, or not given it any special importance. But this circumstance is not pathetic, dramatic, not even bothersome.

In my long life as a journalist, as a political commentator, I have found difficulties that my colleagues did not have; that is, my Catholic colleagues. But they were not insurmountable problems. However, after my experiences in the clandestine prisons of Argentina, it is impossible for me to focus on these problems without being overwhelmed by the difference between Jewish and non-Jewish prisoners.

The struggle for human rights, for tolerance and democracy, against terrorist violence on the extreme Left and the extreme Right, was not easy. And it is true that there was more risk for a Jew, as the defamation campaigns organized by the Argentine government showed. But all that was bearable, that is to say, humanly bearable. Where the difference became unbearable was in the prisons. The humiliations and degradations to which the Jews were subjected, the special corporal punishments given to them, the insults. And at the same time, the world's silent complicity in this degrading discrimination, this degrading pain.

According to an editorial on anti-Semitism in the Buenos Aires *Herald*, "Jews in Argentina take it for granted that if for any reason they go to prison, they will be treated far more harshly than Gentiles."

I don't want to forget, and I will not forgive. And every time I refer in any way to those years I have spent in prisons and the struggle I have confronted, and to the theme of human rights, I cannot help but point out this terrible Jewish destiny. In a situation of murderous and pitiless violence, it is difficult to decide to intervene with only the help of ideas and convictions, without belonging to any political party, without being protected by any organization, simply as an independent journalist. I have experienced it personally. I have seen it in many of my colleagues, Jews and non-Jews— many of them assassinated, imprisoned, or missing. But when in the midst of violence one has to make a decision, being independent and Jewish, knowing how alone one may be in confronting this hatred multiplied by the fact of being Jewish, it is a painful choice.

I am glad I made the decision in time, although during many hours of desperation I felt it would be difficult to keep on meeting the challenge. In any event, we should pay homage to those Jews who have decided to confront the violence of totalitarianism, knowing that in the fight for human rights they will be viewed in terms of their birth as much as their ideas.

Some military friends offered me what they regarded as sound advice: to leave the country for a couple of years until the most violent phase of the repressive process had passed. Turn over the management of the newspaper to my colleagues until the violence is quelled. Or, not publish certain articles. Or, not publish the names of people who disappeared every day. In short, to find some sort of compromise with reality.

This "realism," this pragmatic spirit, is the most important mechanism of survival in a totalitarian country. The biological tendency to survive, manifesting itself in a rationalization of conditioning. A moral, practical, or ideological explanation of the attitudes that have to be acquired in order to survive.

One can say to oneself, my acts aren't going to change history and will lead only to my death; but if I *survive*, I'll be useful in the reconstruction of the country. If I publish the names of the disappeared, as their family members request, I won't prevent them from being killed but will succeed in having myself killed, whereas if I don't publish the names I'll be able to *survive* in order to continue the fight. At such moments as these, nothing I do or print can modify events since the extreme sectors of the armed forces dominate the situation; whereas if I *survive*, I'll be able to help moderate groups with my newspaper when they arrive at a position to assume power.

This conditioning toward reality is continually practiced by the large majority of the population. Whichever example

you choose—Hitler's Germany, Stalin's Russia, Mussolini's
Italy, Castro's Cuba—virtually the entire population will con·
sistently seek a compromise with reality in order to be able
to survive and be useful at a more propitious moment. So
whoever departs from such almost biological pragmatism
becomes suspect not only to those in power but also to the
population in general.

On many occasions the military expressed their admiration
for my open confrontations with the leftist terrorists, whom
I accused in my newspaper and named, using no euphemisms. But they subsequently found it hard to fathom why,
with the same vociferousness, I likewise accused those who
used terrorist methods to liquidate left-wing guerrillas. They
questioned my motives in fighting against military allies, the
right-wing terrorists, and none of my replies provided them
with any satisfaction. They invariably felt that the tactic of
repression was of greater importance than the ideology behind the process.

My newspaper was the one most persecuted by the four
Perónist presidents who ruled Argentina between 1973 and
1976, the most persecuted by Perónism of the Left and the
Right. And there was no way of explaining to the military
that I firmly believed in the need to repress all terrorism, but
that this had to be and could be accomplished within the
legal framework of Argentine law.

The military believed—today they realize the degree to
which they were mistaken—that they would never have to
answer for the extermination policy that was pursued between 1976 and 1980. When the fact emerged that aside from
the independent brand of journalism I practiced, I was also
passionately Jewish and passionately Zionist, all their
schemes collapsed. A kind of panic overcame them, as if they
were in the presence of Satan.

Some fifteen years ago I supported a group of democratic
colonels considered to be the most brilliant men in the army.
Those who discussed their positions used me as an element
of criticism: if Timerman backs them, it surely means they're

incapable of winning; Timerman is goading them to action in order to divide the army.

In 1977 I sent a reporter to a province to write articles on an army general who was doing a superior job of governing. The man was so fearful of being praised by my newspaper that he sent me a telegram saying he didn't want any praise of his administration to be printed, since he was acting totally on behalf of the nation and not in quest of glory.

Some of the military felt that they could understand me as a religious individual or as a religious Zionist. But when I informed them, or printed the fact, that I wasn't an observant Jew but that I was a Jew from a political point of view, and also a political Zionist, they felt a kind of terror before the unknown.

My Judaism was a political act. But Judaism as a political category proved impossible for the military to understand. At the same time there were many other things that were impossible to understand, that proved overly suspect for a mentality educated in anti-Semitism, inclined toward anti-Semitism, or openly anti-Semitic. They couldn't accept or comprehend that an Argentine patriot could simultaneously be a patriotic Jew, a Zionist of the Left, a publisher of psychology books, a defender of Salvador Allende, of the Soviet dissidents, and of political prisoners in Cuban jails. Their world was simpler. And in order to survive in that world, one needed to choose between two extremes. For many, the great majority, it was simple. For me, impossible.

And this too is what made the Jewish leaders of Buenos Aires regard me as an irritating element.

In the pages of my newspaper, all the country's anti-Semitic acts were protested and denounced. The president of the Jewish community, Dr. Nehemias Reznitsky, then explained to me that they ought not all to be protested, for that would create a confrontation with highly powerful sectors of the army. There was a better tactic: to protest some and maintain silence over others, in an attempt to negotiate and survive.

Psychologists were persecuted, democratic priests were persecuted, journalists, university professors, Jews and defense
lawyers of political prisoners, all were persecuted or humiliated. The majority opted for silence, abiding by the new
values that constrained their professions, that denigrated
their creative spirit. The overriding majority accepted this
golden ghetto and survival, the voluptuous sensation of security, that wonderful biological sensation of knowing beyond
a doubt that you're alive.

But if all are guilty of compromising with reality—or
rather, innocent, since it is nearly understandable that life in
any situation or circumstance is preferable to death—why
should I have this obsession only about the complicity of the
Jewish leaders in Argentina?

After the war, we began to fathom the magnitude of the
Holocaust. And we promised ourselves that never again
would this silent, methodical destruction of our people be
repeated. We also promised ourselves, and swore repeatedly
through the years, that never again would our own silence,
passivity, confusion, and paralysis be repeated. We promised
ourselves that never would horror paralyze us, intimidate us,
allow us to develop theories of survival, of compromise with
reality, of delaying our public indignation.

The point of reference for the Jewish leaders of Buenos
Aires, as for Jewish leaders in many parts of the world, is the
horror of the Holocaust. A gas chamber, a concentration
camp, a selection made in front of crematorium ovens, is the
point of reference that must determine whether the moment for total and open battle against anti-Semitism has
arrived.

For me, the point of reference is equally the responsibility
of Jews in the face of any anti-Semitic act. The point of reference is Jewish action; the Jewish silence of the Hitler years
toward Hitler's acts.

I was never able to understand how the horrors of the

Holocaust could diminish the significance of the violation of Jewish girls in clandestine Argentine prisons. I was never able to accept how recalling and recording the activity of the Holocaust industry could render it seemingly unnecessary to confront openly the publication of anti-Semitic literature in Argentina and the fact that such literature is studied in the military academies of Buenos Aires.

To my mind, always, the incorporation of the Holocaust into my life meant never to allow the Argentine police to feel that they were authorized to humiliate Jewish prisoners. I never imagined that there would be Jewish leaders who would utilize the horrors of the Holocaust to maintain that the most advantageous response to ce tain anti-Semitic aggressions of a much less brutal nature was silence.

Thus, in my opinion the most important lesson of the Holocaust doesn't lie in the horrors committed by Naziism. Expounding those over and over fails to move any anti-Semite to pity. But the Holocaust teaches us the need to understand the Jewish silence and the Jewish incapacity to defend itself; it lies in the Jewish incapacity to confront the world with its own insanity, with the significance of anti-Semitic insanity.

The Holocaust will be understood not so much for the number of victims as for the magnitude of the silence. And what obsesses me most is the repetition of silence rather than the possibility of another Holocaust.

The Jewish leaders of Argentina are trying to measure the impending danger by the magnitude of anti-Semitic acts. They are attempting to locate in their memories, fears, and beliefs some table of values that will enable them to predict the future, that will indicate how many Jewish schools must be bombed, how many anti-Semitic programs transmitted, how much anti-Semitic propaganda published for the trend to be regarded as of Holocaust proportions. Whereas I, using my newspaper as a base, fought so that not even the slightest anti-Semitic trace should be left in silence, for the silence of the Jews is the sole indicator of the current presence of the Holocaust in the Jewish historical condition.

. . .

The balcony of my house in a suburb of Tel Aviv faces the
Mediterranean. It is large, almost the size of a room, and my
wife has filled it with flowers, plants, and Max Ernst posters.
Facing my balcony, the scarlet sun is sinking over a sea that's
too blue for my eyes, which are accustomed to the southern
Atlantic. It hasn't rained in Tel Aviv for nine months, and the
ceremony of the sun blazing over the sea is repeated daily.
This is a peculiarly odd moment in my life. Pity emerges as
stronger than my memory, and more tender than my ideology. I think of those Jewish leaders in Buenos Aires, trying to
find a point of equilibrium between their terror and paralysis
and the anticipated pardon from the moderate military. I
recall a time when they felt proud that a powerful Timerman
was propounding in his newspaper such strong Judaism and
Zionism, discoursing on an equal footing with the military,
the Catholic Church, politicians, union leaders. They felt
protected. Timerman's downfall aroused the feelings deeply
hidden in the subconscious of every Jew: the fear of leaving
the medieval ghetto limits at night and of being unable,
within those dark, narrow streets, to have recourse to the
protection of the feudal lord.

How can one fail to feel pity for them? After all, wasn't it
a sheer accident that the military dictatorship organized the
largest scandal ever launched in Argentina against Jews who
considered themselves the equal of other citizens? The
greatest anti-Semitic act was silencing those who were not
afraid to speak up. A silent, frightened Jewry. A Jewry that
has once again found it necessary to make a pragmatic compromise with reality by way of silence. One could not ask for
a greater victory for Argentine anti-Semitism: a Jewry at a
loss as to what to do, unaware of what lies in store, unaware
of its strength or the strength of the enemy.

It is possible to feel pity and it is possible to feel rage. Both
feelings are the result of love. And how can one fail to love
this tortured, sacrificed people, who are abandoned each

time that history becomes very complicated and dangerous for them?

In the clandestine jail of Puesto Vasco, headed by Colonel Ramón Camps, a woman is tortured. My cell is very close to the kitchen where the torture is applied. I can hear her clearly, crying out, shouting that she isn't a Jew, that her name is German. There's nothing simpler for an Argentine policeman than to confuse names that are odd-sounding to him. But here in Tel Aviv, facing the Jewish Mediterranean, I think about that scene, that had she been a Jew, she wouldn't have had even that last line of defense. What loneliness! And I also think that if she was lying, and actually was Jewish, what a terrible renunciation.

In the clandestine prison of Coti Martínez, which was under the supervision of General Guillermo Suárez Mason, a man of about seventy is being beaten by a policeman. The man's hands are tied behind his back and his eyes are blindfolded. The policeman pulls off the cross the man is wearing around his neck and accuses him of being a Jew, of wanting to hide his identity. After his beating, the old man is put into my cell, and he tells me that he converted to Catholicism nearly fifty years ago and that the cross was a gift from Pope Paul VI. He considers himself a Catholic and is enraged that they do not believe him. He vows to avenge himself on the gray-haired policeman with the small, pudgy hands who beat him and who passes our cell every day smiling.

And here, facing the Jewish Mediterranean, I think about that old man, eternally Jewish in my eyes, who was beaten as a Jew, and that Catholic woman who was beaten as a Jew, about those two Catholics beaten as Jews because they were hated as Jews, and I suppose that I no longer have a right to demand anything of any Jew. What people, what individual, can withstand such hatred? How can one demand anyone to exercise such a superhuman effort so that his right to life is respected, to have the strength to live if he barely has the strength to allow himself to be led to death?

Yet—once again that *yet*—is there perhaps any other

human group, any other people, that incurs such a risk in not confronting their enemies as the Jews? In Argentina, in 1980, thirty-five years after Hitler's defeat, on the army-controlled television channel in Buenos Aires, one heard the following questions voiced by a journalist who has practiced his profession for twenty years and is not naïve, the brother of a general who heads the press services of the military government: Why aren't there any poor Jews? Why do Jews give so much money to Israel? Why don't Jews marry Catholics? Why do Jews consider themselves superior?

A repetition of the insults and defamations of Nazi rulers, stemming from one of the most powerful forces in Argentine life, the army. It's easy enough to react to this anti-Semitic campaign, to feel offended, to have no hesitation in identifying this journalist, whose name is Llamas de Madariaga.

It's easy to recognize an anti-Semite. It is more complicated to recognize an anti-Semitic situation. It ought not to be, since the Jews for hundreds of years have found themselves faced with similar situations. Yet—once again *yet*—it isn't easy to live in a country and have to accuse the army of indirectly fostering anti-Semitism. And it's harder still to denounce liberals who, as in all countries that succumb to anti-Semitic totalitarianism of the Left or the Right, lend their service not to anti-Semites but to the anti-Semitic situation in general.

Máximo Gainza, the head of the Buenos Aires newspaper *La Prensa,* is a liberal, a democratic man. His newspaper reported that I had received the award given by the International Federation of Newspaper Publishers, the Golden Pen of Freedom of 1980, and also the Arthur Morse Award from the Aspen Institute. These are two of the most distinguished awards in international journalism. Only one Argentine journalist before myself received the former award, Máximo Gainza's own father, the late Alberto Gainza Paz. Neither of these two institutions is Jewish. In addition, I have also received awards from the United Jewish Appeal, the American Jewish Committee, the Anti-Defamation League of Bnai

Brith, Hadassah, and the United Synagogue of America. And yet this liberal man, in statements to a Buenos Aires magazine, indicated that I had received "two or three awards, all given by Jewish organizations."

Reading this, how easy it is to conclude that there exists a worldwide Jewish conspiracy, that Jews give awards to Jews for mutual support. Clearly a liberal man like Máximo Gainza doesn't believe this. The curious thing is that he says it without believing it, that he allows this conclusion to be reached without bothering to say it directly, leaving the task of such interpretation to the Nazis.

It's a psychological and ideological process we've seen repeated many times in the history of this century: adjusting to a situation without sharing its ideas leads inevitably to being an accomplice of the acts engendered by those ideas.

Máximo Gainza is not an anti-Semite, and his newspaper will defend the Jews. Yet he will be used as an instrument by anti-Semites because he has been dragged into the situation. Máximo Gainza knows that the International Federation of Newspaper Publishers which cited his father some years ago is not a Jewish organization. But he remains silent on that identification. He remains silent exactly the way the anti-Semites require him to, leading public opinion to believe that my struggle for freedom of the press has been recognized only by Jews. And if only Jews were awarding a Jew, the whole matter became suspect.

Again, once again, the Jew is a man under total suspicion.

11

When they broke into the house, they didn't find the one they were looking for, the father. They placed hoods over the others and took them away—the mother, both sons, the daughter-in-law, and the servant. A few days later the servant was released. They began torturing the mother, the sons, and daughter-in-law. Whereupon the father appeared before a judge to testify that it was he who the police were after and that he was turning himself over to the hands of justice. The judge turned him over to the police, and the police released his wife.

The father, the sons, and the daughter-in-law were incarcerated at Coti Martínez, the clandestine prison. For a while all four were tortured. Then only the father. Before each of the father's torture sessions, his sons were ordered to prepare food for him and take care of him so that he'd be fortified for the torture. The father was tied to the bed with an iron ring, and ate with his other hand, assisted by his sons and daughter-in-law. The three would then say goodbye to him, trying to bolster his spirits for the torture session.

If we were to leave the scene at this juncture, we might ask ourselves which universe, country, and period does it belong to? How does this scene conceivably differ from the events that transpired during the period of Mussolini, Hitler, Franco, Stalin? In certain procedural details, perhaps, though not in the conception of the event. For the event was conceived in accordance with a basic totalitarian principle: A political deed can be achieved through the destruction of an individual; violence committed upon one person can signify the solution of a political problem, the strengthening of an ideology, a system.

If this scene were printed in Russian, would anyone doubt that it had occurred in some remote region of the USSR? And if written in German, would it differ in any way from the episodes that occurred repeatedly during the consolidation process of the Hitler regime, the suppression of opponents and personal enemies of the regime's hierarchy, or the result of intrigues arising between various leaders of the regime?

The scene actually took place in Argentina and involved the Miralles family. The father had been Minister of Economics to a provincial Perónist governor, and had fought alongside army moderates against leftist Perónist guerrillas and in support of Isabel Perón's overthrow. This governor, Victorio Calabró, might become in the future a leader who was favorable to a moderate military that wanted to win the Perónist vote. The most probable candidate, General Roberto Viola, then chief of the Army General Staff, was guaranteeing Calabró's security against kidnapping. The hard line, pursued by Generals Ibérico Saint Jean, Guillermo Suárez Mason, and Ramón J. Camps, sought to destroy Viola and his potential future aspirations, and thereby Calabró as well, whose leadership had its origins in the union world. Since kidnapping Calabró was impossible, the other alternative was to put him on trial, accuse him of some crime. Hence, a charge had to be found, and nothing certainly could serve this purpose better than questioning his Minister of Economics in order to prove illegal profiteering.

If this story of intrigues were framed solely in political language, it would be no different from countless accounts in a democracy. A group of conservatives attempts to find arguments that will invalidate the potential future candidacy of a liberal or moderate military leader. That is democracy. What transforms this into a Hitlerian episode is that the methods assume precedence over the goals. And that, in brief, is the clue to Argentina: rulers who declare democratic goals, refuse to be accused of having other goals, go to great pains to receive international journalists and declare that their aims are the reconstruction of Argentine democracy. Yet when the actual mechanisms that govern Argentine life begin to emerge, the situation is no different than the one in prewar Germany between 1933 and 1939.

I was imprisoned with the Miralles family at Coti Martínez, and afterwards at Puesto Vasco with the father and one of his sons. Many times I heard the father, after prolonged torture, crying out that he would sign whatever was demanded, pleading to be killed. But the fact remained that he couldn't provide any incriminating evidence against Calabró, for there was none. Several months later he was released.

Of all the dramatic situations I witnessed in clandestine prisons, nothing can compare to those family groups who were tortured often together, sometimes separately but in view of one another, or in different cells, while one was aware of the other being tortured. The entire affective world, constructed over the years with utmost difficulty, collapses with a kick in the father's genitals, a smack on the mother's face, an obscene insult to the sister, or the sexual violation of a daughter. Suddenly an entire culture based on familial love, devotion, the capacity for mutual sacrifice collapses. Nothing is possible in such a universe, and that is precisely what the torturers know.

The father's glances: of desperation at first, then of apology, and then of encouragement. Seeking some way to mutually help one another—sending an apple, a glass of water. Those fathers, thrown on the ground, bleeding, endeavoring for their children to find the strength to resist the tortures still in store for them. The impotence, that impotence that arises not from one's failure to do something in defense of one's children but from one's inability to extend a tender gesture. From my cell, I'd hear the whispered voices of children trying to learn what was happening to their parents, and I'd witness the efforts of daughters to win over a guard, to arouse a feeling of tenderness in him, to incite the hope of some lovely future relationship between them in order to learn what was happening to her mother, to have an orange sent to her, to get permission for her to go to the bathroom.

Those family groups, destroyed and crushed together, without the hope that comes from thinking about others on the outside, as I was able to do with regard to my wife and children. Those fathers, devoid of heroism, desperate to provide the answers the torturers were after, but often uninformed about the matter, ignorant of the intrigue that was unfolding around them with them at its center. It was the true end of the civilization I'd been reared in, because it marked the disappearance of what was once the family; consolation was impossible, tenderness untenable, protection violated in every form. The old protective, tender family was vanishing, to give way to a group that was unable to express anything toward one another that possessed any force, validity, or semblance of utility. It all wound up in a fresh moan from a beloved person being tortured, and once again only madness provided some escape from the collapse of a life that had begun with love, was based on tenderness, and ought to have been enveloped in solidarity.

An old one-story house in the village of Martínez, twenty kilometers north of Buenos Aires. Formerly a police station. There is a narrow entrance and an entry gate for automobiles. A small anteroom of the house serves as depot for weapons and leads into another small room with two bunk beds, the guard's bedroom. Both give out on a narrow, short passageway with a door going into the office of intelligence and files. This is followed by another room, the chief's office, and still another room that has a private bathroom and two beds—the bedroom of the two chief officers and, when the kitchen is occupied, the torture chamber. This bedroom and the guard's bedroom both face a square yard, in the middle of which stands a narrow tin shed where prisoners are held for hours or days, either standing, lying down, or tied to a chair. One of the kitchen doors opens on this yard, and another leads into an additional bedroom with bunk beds for the ten men who comprise the police garrison. A door off this bedroom leads into another yard, where there's a common bathroom and a door at the far end leading into a basement. In the basement is a corridor lined with several cells. Here, prisoners are enclosed. The walls are perpetually damp, though some cells are fortunately provided with a hole in the ground. The prisoners in the other cells that lack this provision must ask the guard to accompany them to the bathroom in the yard, which the guard is not always willing to do. One of the cells with a hole hasn't been opened up for a year. They say a guerrilla is inside. The cells have no numbers, the prisoners have no names, in this clandestine prison operated by General Guillermo Suárez Mason and known as Coti Martínez.

I am in the guard's bedroom off the first passageway, tied to the bed after the beating given me the day I was brought from police headquarters in Buenos Aires. All the cells are occupied, and I am being detained either because no clear instructions regarding my disposition have been received or they've been delayed. No one knows why I'm here. I've already been tortured, questioned in April and May of 1977, and now June and July have arrived. They're intrigued. Afterwards, orders are received that I'm to be held but not molested. Never have they had a similar case, and don't quite know what it bodes for the future. Each in his own way tries to establish some sort of dialogue with me. They imagine that one day I'll again be in charge of a newspaper. They're professionals, and wouldn't like me, due to some twist in politics, to get involved in their persecution.

A guard asks me for work for one of his sons who doesn't

want to study. A boy of fourteen who's causing him problems, and whom he'd like to have learn a good trade. I recommend a trade school, and despite the fact of my disappearance, he isn't worried about visiting the director of this school and using my name to apply for an opening for his son. He doesn't feel he's doing anything incorrect, and goes on to explain that it's all simply a matter of preventing thieves—at first he says Jews, but then corrects himself—from carrying off Argentina's money. He has his morals: When sent by his chief to find a terrorist, he will kill the man and others with him— wife, parents, children—only if resistance is offered; but if the terrorist doesn't resist, he's brought to the chief. Only if the chief issues the order does the guard place the revolver at the prisoner's neck and kill him. He doesn't kill for pleasure, only out of necessity or in obedience to an order. There are others, he says, who do it for pleasure or in a sporting spirit, competing with the others in the number of *enfriados,* the captives who wind up as "cold bodies." He's a nice man, who looks after his diet, brings his utensils from home because he thinks the ones in the kitchen are contaminated, hopes to be able to retire soon while still young, for since his job is dangerous the years of service are calculated as double. When his chiefs are not around, he lets me use their bathroom.

There's always someone who comes to chat with me. Gradually, my situation is eased. I'm no longer chained to the bed night and day, only at night, and eventually this too is abandoned. I'm allowed to walk in the yard, providing there's a guard in sight. Above the house stands a tower occupied by two men with machine guns. The food at first is extremely poor; afterwards I'm offered what the guards eat. Some of the prisoners are wealthy, and once their interrogations and torture are over, they enjoy special status if able to pay the officers a daily sum. They're allowed to cook, wash their clothes, and some are permitted to talk to their families on the telephone.

I'm continually asked why I'm here. I don't know, nor do

they. The only order they have is to take care of me. I have a number, without a name, but my picture has appeared in the newspapers so many times that no one is ignorant of my identity. At times some of the prisoners are taken out into the courtyard, whereupon I must remain in my cell room, though I can see them through the windows.

Discipline at the beginning is always rigid, then as the days pass it becomes lax. By now, I think all the prisoners are aware of my presence, aside from those who've been enclosed for a year or two in underground cells without permission to leave. I get to know prisoners, and can't help hearing the remarks of the police or military about each one. Some had relatives who'd paid a ransom, assuming that the kidnapping had been committed by criminals. In certain cases, the men were allowed to leave after the ransom was received; in others, they were killed despite receipt of the money. The ransom is regarded as a means of financing the operations and existence of this parallel army, without having to touch government funds. When a sum is collected, there's great rejoicing and a celebration party, leading me to suspect that the money is divided among everybody. This is what happened with the huge stipend paid by Rafael Perrota's family to obtain his release. Judging by the attention given to this elderly journalist, the efforts at concealing him here at Coti Martínez from the view of others, there never was any intention of granting his freedom. In any event, a decision was awaited from Colonel Ramón Camps or General Suárez Mason whether to release or to kill him.

The guards possess other privileges that are revealed in these close quarters once you gain a certain measure of freedom and overhear their conversations. Coti Martínez is located in a northern suburb of Buenos Aires that has a night life. The torturers and their officers are entitled to control over prostitution in certain bars, to exploit some of the women, and to enjoy impunity in their protection of secret gambling operators.

Three very beautiful girls are inmates at Coti Martínez and

service the guards' sexual whims. The girls, accused of terrorism, are quite young, between twenty and twenty-two perhaps. They've been tortured, violated, and gradually cor-
rupted, out of that need a prisoner experiences of building
some sort of life that encompasses a measure of hope, some
natural connection with life, some sort of reality besides the
flight into madness or suicide. These inmates want to live,
and they accept the lives of their torturers rather than resign
themselves to the life of the tortured, or of the isolated in-
mate, that ghost who's been in a cell for a year and can be
heard coughing day and night. Curious relationships are established: one of the girls, the chief's lover, managed to obtain authorization for her father to come and live with her.
Both occupy the same cell, and the father wound up being
friends with his daughter's lover. The father is an electrical
engineer and attends to all the needs at Coti Martínez, especially those related to lights and the machines used in applying electric shocks. He goes out to do the shopping, brings me
an orange, sometimes serves me a piece of meat with my
meal.

It's a world for those who are either resigned or mad. I
haven't the slightest notion what I'm doing here with my
baggage of meditation, identification with the Holocaust,
predictions on the inevitable future, that inevitable triumph
of truth, democracy, human rights. Sometimes I engage the
guards on these subjects—and they don't know what to do.
Normally, I would have been beaten for expressing such
things, but they lack instructions.

At night, the torture sessions take place, and music is
turned on to block out the outcries of those who are being
tortured. In the morning, I'm asked if I heard anything. Occasionally, in the midst of a torture session, someone will
need a fact, and I will be sent for. When did Lenin say such
and such a thing? When did Herzl decide to build a Jewish
state in Uganda? Who was Minister of Defense during such
and such an Argentine government?

They're glad when I'm taken away from this place. One of

them cracks a joke: *Once you're free, you'll order us all killed.*

The reason for my removal from this location is an impending visit from Benjamin Gilman, an American congressman who's taken an interest in my situation. I'm brought to the Government Building where Gilman has an interview with the president of the Republic. I'm warned that my conversation with Gilman will be taped, whereupon I realize that it isn't me who's being threatened, but my wife and children. So, there we are in the Government Building in Buenos Aires, with Benjamin Gilman questioning me with his eyes in the presence of an Argentine official, while I try to speak to him with my eyes. Those glances, comprehensible only to those who at some point have had to employ their gaze in like manner, using their eyes in ways for which there are no words, for which adequately explanatory words do not exist. Only glances.

Just as there are no words to conceive of the message in that father's eyes as he departed from his sons at the hour of torture. The torture of all.

When the Argentine armed forces seized power in March 1976, they had already developed an entire philosophy of repression. As they plunged into full-scale repression, unleashed their madness, and began discovering that that repression in its daily manifestation conformed to the similar picture of other massacres, they realized that the verdict awaiting them would be no different than the verdict previously applied to earlier massacres.

The Argentine military at present perceive the Nuremberg Trials in the Latin American context not as a historic event but as an actual possibility. They still feel justified historically, but foresee the improbability of being pardoned by their contemporaries. They still believe that history will validate their personal destinies, but fear that in their lifetime they may be individually vulnerable.

It's curious, the extent to which the recent years in Argentina have repeated—in a different geographical context, another culture, another period, another calendar moment—the world of terror, hatred, madness, and delirium that governed the Hitlerian epoch in Germany.

At the approach of the anticipated end of the satanic explosion that had been unleashed in Europe, many German hierarchs sought refuge in mystical explanations of their historic role vis-à-vis mankind. At present, the Argentine military is engaged in attempting to convince mankind that it was the first to confront World War III, the decisive struggle against leftist terrorism.

The Nazis believed that it was their obligation to carry the war to its ultimate lengths, for such methods—regardless of their cruelty—were imposed upon them by the historical destiny they were fulfilling. The members of the Argentine military claim impunity in the unleashing of brutality, insisting that the war against terrorism was imposed upon them, in which case methods matter less than destiny. Cruelty is an accessory mechanism requiring neither justification nor explanation. This common denominator of the existence of horror as one's voluntary acceptance of an imposed destiny emerged with the same characteristics in Germany in the thirties and in Argentina in the seventies.

In Nazi Germany, the Jews were guilty through birth, the liberals through weakness and corruption, the Communists through ideology. The same equation of guilt proved suitable for the enemy of the Argentine military.

The Nazis' protest to the world was that their struggle had not been understood. They asked for world understanding regarding their national sacrifice against mankind's common enemy. The members of the Argentine military are convinced that what they label the anti-Argentine campaign is the sole factor that has prevented the modern world from understanding the service they're rendering mankind. They hold this "anti-Argentine campaign" responsible for focusing world attention on the tortured, the prisoners, the disappeared, rather than on the fact that Argentina is the ground where terrorism for the first time is being mercilessly defeated.

The Argentine military members, like the German Nazi rulers, have succeeded in reducing opposition to their theories to a minimum within their own land. As in Germany, those individuals who are untouched by repression, violence, and irrationality are happy. As in Germany, they are the majority. And, as in Germany, they enjoy the benefits of an order erected by those who give orders, for those who adjust to the established order.

German Jews, between 1933 and 1938, were convinced that things would improve, and they waited. They loved their homes and habits; they felt that they were German. Argentine Jews, untouched by irrationality, are annoyed when questioned about Jews who have disappeared, about the treatment of Jewish prisoners, the photographs of Hitler in clandestine prisons and barracks. German Jews maintained that it was still possible to resolve the problem; Argentine Jews contend that the experiences taking place do not constitute a policy but are the exception. Episodes of anti-Semitic hostility represent isolated outbursts of feelings among certain military leaders, not a philosophy or even an ideology.

Some German liberals went into hiding during Naziism, a very few; others escaped the country. The majority tried to become faceless in order to survive inside Germany. Argentine liberals are also trying to survive, imagining that the absence of a specific denunciation of the crimes being committed will facilitate a solution of common agreement with other military officials. The result is a complicity, Argentine style, similar to the complicity that prevailed in Germany among those who claimed unawareness of what was happening.

The Germans considered those who denounced Nazi crimes abroad as traitors. The Argentine military consider it anti-Argentine of those who are abroad to signal this incredible phenomenon of a civilized, educated country in the late seventies repeating the same incredible universe, the same perversion of human nature as overcame Germany forty years ago.

It is not, therefore, the number of horrors, the lengthy enumeration of crimes committed, the analysis of methods used in combating leftist terrorism, or the elaboration of methods that might have been employed without recourse to state terrorism; it is not the clarification of the role played by state terrorism, nor the perverse, aggressive inclination of the Argentine military toward anti-Semitism that constitutes the key to recent years in Argentina.

Nor is it the analysis and study of that anti-Semitic tendency which was openly displayed in a series of carefully laid scandals against prominent Jews, accusations never confirmed by facts; nor the dedication of Argentine Jewish community leaders to concealing these facts from international public opinion by disguising them as exceptional and isolated situations. Despite the fact that the Argentine military, as in Germany, has seized banks, business firms, jewelry, property, and furnishings belonging to persecuted Jews.

Nor does the key to Argentina, the interesting aspect of the Argentine case, reside in the fact that—as in totalitarian countries—most of the press was able to survive and preferred to do so by allying itself with that anti-Semitic, anti-democratic psychological warfare, that total concealment of crimes, by diverting attention to other realities, feigning an ignorance which at some future point could justify and prove total innocence.

No, in my opinion, the key to the present moment, to that profound mystery, lies elsewhere. How can a nation reproduce in every detail, though employing other forms, in every argument, though employing other words, the same monstrous crimes explicitly condemned and clearly expounded so many years before? That is the Argentine mystery: the fact that the world has been unable to avoid something seemingly destroyed forever in 1945, in the ashes of Berlin, in the gallows of the Nuremberg Trials, and in the United Nations Charter. The fact that, in the 1970s, a nation of no great importance, undergoing an explosion of lustful, murderous drives, has found coexistence with the world at large, without need of ideology and without need of despair. Merely as a bad hangover of that bygone period, and a forewarning that these hangovers still prevail and can recur, time and again, with barely a trace of hope.

Epilogue

The police in the clandestine prisons liked to joke. It was a form of omnipotence that consisted of converting a situation of horror into one of diversion. When a political prisoner was led to the torture chamber, they used to comment among themselves: will he sing an opera or a tango? If scant information was obtained, it was a tango. When it was a Jewish prisoner, the jokes would refer to the gas chambers, to Auschwitz—"We'll show the Nazis how to do things." Omnipotence likewise surfaced in the forms of consolation. "Well, don't worry, you only die once." And always, seemingly normal forms of humiliation. For example, gathering all the prisoners of a clandestine jail into a single room, throwing one on top of another, the men and women trying to guess their individual fates through some gesture of the guards, all this under the pretext of having to make a general cleanup.

Despite this, whenever someone was being prepared for transfer, his eyes blindfolded, his hands tied behind him, thrown on the ground in back of a car and covered with a blanket, he would have preferred to remain in the clandestine prison. You never knew whether you were being led to an interrogation, torture, death, or another prison where once again you'd have to discover the pathetic mechanisms of survival.

When newspapers began publishing rumors that I was to be transferred to my home and kept under house arrest, the Israeli and U.S. embassies in Buenos Aires were afraid that this decision might be an invitation to extremist sectors of the armed forces to try to liquidate me before the transfer could take place. American diplomats informed my wife that they were considering a scheme whereupon at the moment of my transfer, which would certainly be kept secret, I should declare myself ill, simulate a heart attack or whatever, and request the presence of a well-known doctor. In this way, they could have exact knowledge of the event, could place an ambulance at my wife's disposal, and would be in a position to control the situation to some degree. This was not necessary, although the transfer to my home possessed all the elements of anguish and terror.

I had been under arrest for thirty months when the Buenos Aires newspapers began to publish the account. The Supreme Court would order the government to arrange for my release since there was no indictment against me. Although the military tribunal, in September 1977, declared that there were no charges against me and that I was free, I remained under house arrest by order of the military junta. A curious episode occurred. The legal adviser to the Jewish institutions in Buenos Aires claimed that my arrest was not illegal inasmuch as the Supreme Court had not been disobeyed: the Court had ordered my release from the president, but not from the military junta.

Finally, in September 1979, the Supreme Court again convened, and it was assumed that my release would be ordered. When this decision was taken, instead of my wife or attorney being informed, as befits judicial procedure, the government was told of the decision and kept it secret. The generals, in special session, decided that despite the Court order, I would not be released. The Supreme Court threatened to resign. The generals were prepared to arrest the Court. The president of Argentina, General Videla, declared that if the Court resigned, he too would present his resignation. My wife was in Washington working with a group of congressmen who were putting intense pressure on the Argentine government; the Vatican was also investigating the matter—at which point, I underwent the final transfer.

It's Tuesday morning. The Buenos Aires newspapers report that there's agitation at army headquarters, and that high-ranking officers are discussing what position to take toward the Supreme Court's decision to order my release. Meetings of the military junta are being announced. It is said that on Wednesday there will be a definitive meeting at which the generals will put my case to a vote.

It is Tuesday noon, and Rabbi Roberto Graetz, a member of the Permanent Assembly of Human Rights, visits me. He now lives in Rio de Janeiro since two attempts have been made on his life in Buenos Aires. He has noticed a considerable increase of policemen around my house, and tells me he had trouble entering. His wife has sent me a cake. They allow him to come into my apartment for five minutes only, then he leaves.

An hour later a high police official arrives. I've never seen him before. He's accompanied by the police chief of the zone in which my house is located. He says he's going to move me elsewhere, where I'm to sign some papers. I'm to take a bag with some clothing. I refuse, and insist on being told where I'm going, or that my lawyer or rabbi be called. He says that if I don't go peaceably, I'll be taken by force. I argue, the telephone rings, he answers and says that he's leaving now. He hangs up and insists that he's in a hurry. I'm alone in the apartment and upset because there is no witness to my transfer.

We descend in an elevator filled with policemen and go down to the basement of the building where a private car without any police markings is waiting for us. I'm told to

take the back seat. There's a great display of plainclothes-
men. In the car I'm seated alongside a young, elegantly
dressed woman. I ask her if she too is a prisoner; she tells
me she's a policewoman. We drive quickly, escorted by several private cars filled with civilians. They try to avoid being
recognized.

At the federal security offices I'm informed that I have
been stripped of my citizenship and expelled from the country, and will be transported at once to the airport. I argue
that this decision is illegal since only a judge can take such
a measure, and that in order for it to be valid, sixty days must
elapse during which I have the right to appeal. "Appeal from
Israel," I'm told by the Assistant to the Minister of the Interior. So I learn that I'm to go to Israel. I'm handed a passport,
which is valid for only two days. Then the Israeli chargé
d'affaires comes into the room and attaches the visa to my
passport. He insists on accompanying me. A brief argument
ensues, during which he states that he won't let me go alone,
that he wishes to accompany me to the plane. We all leave
the building together. They keep arguing. Israeli security
men are waiting on the ground floor, where two automobiles
are parked. The atmosphere is extremely tense. A police
official indicates that we'll be going to a heliport since a
helicopter will be taking me to the airport, which is thirty
kilometers from the city, and that the Israeli official can fol-
low us in his own car.

Once in the heliport, the Israeli security men again insist
on accompanying me to the plane. Then a high-ranking official says that no one can join the individuals on my helicopter, but a second helicopter will be escorting us in the event
of an attack from land, and the chargé d'affaires can go in that
one.

We reach the airport, where an Aerolineas Argentinas
plane destined for Rome is waiting. We get into the plane
along with the airport commander, a patrol of air force soldiers, and the Israeli official—my companions. The individuals escorting me leave, the Israeli diplomat going last, so as

to be certain that the door is closed and I remain on the plane. The plane takes off.

Some time later, I learned from my wife that the U.S. Embassy had passage prepared for me on an American plane and a group of security officers ready to transfer me to Washington. I also found out that during the airplane stops—at Rio de Janeiro, Madrid, Rome—police from various countries observed my presence in order to prevent any assault.

And I discovered from an article in an Argentine newspaper that fifteen minutes after the departure from my house, a group of military men arrived intending to kidnap me. On the helicopter trip, one policeman told me they had been unable to inform me at my house of my expulsion from the country because various security services had installed wiretapping devices that could have revealed I was leaving the country alive.

I've been in Israel for two days, and am spending Yom Kippur in the Ein Shemer kibbutz where one of my sons lives. I listen to the radio and hear my name and Argentina mentioned, along with that of General Menéndez. I don't understand Hebrew. Someone translates for me: General Menéndez, head of the principal military association, has begun a revolution in an attempt to overthrow the government because of my release.

Since my reflexes are still attuned to Argentina, this gives me a scare. It seems real, plausible, inevitable. I had a feeling that I couldn't escape. And yet General Menéndez, who had acted like a god, who by a mere gesture could rule on the life or death of countless people in the concentration camp of "La Perla," which he headed, was unable to reach me. He could still plunge Argentina into civil war, he could still dispatch numerous Argentines to torture chambers, crematorium ovens, throw them to the bottom of lakes, but he could no longer touch me. Or rather, his paranoia was within hand's reach, though he himself was unable to harm me.

And it is with this sensation—of being distant from the Nazi paranoia that suddenly overcame the most advanced nation of Latin America, as it once overcame the most advanced nation of Europe—that I come to the end of my story.

I know there ought to be a message or a conclusion. But that would be a way of putting a concluding period on a typical story of this century, my story, and I have no concluding period. I have lost none of my anxieties, none of my ideology, none of my love or my hate.

I know too that the Argentine nation will not cease to weep for its dead, because throughout its often brutal history, it has remained loyal to its tragedies. I know that it will succeed in overcoming the paranoids of every extreme, the cowards of every sector. And it will learn how to be happy.

Have any of you ever looked into the eyes of another person, on the floor of a cell, who knows that he's about to die though no one has told him so? He knows that he's about to die but clings to his biological desire to live, as a single hope, since no one has told him that he's to be executed.

I have many such gazes imprinted upon me.

Each time I write or utter words of hope, words of confidence in the definitive triumph of man, I'm fearful—fearful of losing sight of one of those gazes. At night I recount them, recall them, re-see them, cleanse them, illumine them.

Those gazes, which I encountered in the clandestine prisons of Argentina and which I've retained one by one, were the culminating point, the purest moment of my tragedy.

They are here with me today. And although I might wish to do so, I could not and would not know how to share them with you.